SpringerBriefs in Computer Science

Series Editors

Stan Zdonik
Peng Ning
Shashi Shekhar
Jonathan Katz
Xindong Wu
Lakhmi C. Jain
David Padua
Xuemin Shen
Borko Furht
V. S. Subrahmanian
Martial Hebert
Katsushi Ikeuchi
Bruno Siciliano

T0234325

For further volumes:
http://www.springer.com/series/10028

Heng Yin • Dawn Song

Automatic Malware Analysis

An Emulator Based Approach

 Springer

Heng Yin
Department of Electrical Engineering
  and Computer Science
Syracuse University
Syracuse, NY, USA

Dawn Song
Computer Science Division
University of California, Berkeley
Berkeley, CA, USA

This book contains copyright materials from ACM and ISOC

ISSN 2191-5768   ISSN 2191-5776 (electronic)
ISBN 978-1-4614-5522-6   ISBN 978-1-4614-5523-3 (eBook)
DOI 10.1007/978-1-4614-5523-3
Springer New York Heidelberg Dordrecht London

Library of Congress Control Number: 2012945632

Printed on acid-free paper

Springer is part of Springer Science+Business Media (www.springer.com)

Acknowledgements

We acknowledge the contribution made by the past and current members of the BitBlaze team, which is led by Professor Dawn Song at University of California, Berkeley, for analyzing program binaries for security applications. In addition to the authors of this book, other past and current members, including David Brumley, Juan Caballero, Cody Hartwig, Ivan Jager, Min Gyung Kang, Zhenkai Liang, James Newsome, Pongsin Poosankam, Prateek Saxena, have also made contributions to this book.

Contents

Chapter 1
Introduction

1.1 Malware is a Persistent and Growing Threat

Malicious software, i.e., *malware*, is a generic terminology for software with malicious intents. It includes many categories, such as virus, spyware, rootkits, trojan horses, backdoor, bots, etc. Malware has become a severe threat to interconnected computer systems for decades. Some study shows that malware causes billions of dollars financial losses annually [10]. The situation is becoming worse, because malware writers are profit driven. The attackers have incentives to rapidly develop large number of new malware samples and new variants (in the order of thousands or even more per day). To thwart malware detection and analysis, the attackers are actively striving for more and more sophisticated and stealthy attack techniques.

1.2 We Need Automatic Malware Analysis

To fight against the break-neck speed of malware development and innovation, the first thing we need to do is to "know the enemy". Given an unknown and likely malicious binary program, we aim to detect and analyze its malicious behaviors, . This suspicious program can be collected through honeypots, computer forensics of compromised systems, and underground channels. By analyzing this unknown program, we identify its malicious behaviors and extract attack mechanisms. Then we can rely on the analysis results to build up proper defense, such as creating detection signatures and updating detection policies. This analysis process has to be automatic in order to catch up with the speed of malware development.

H. Yin and D. Song, *Automatic Malware Analysis: An Emulator Based Approach*,
SpringerBriefs in Computer Science, DOI 10.1007/978-1-4614-5523-3_1,
© The Author(s) 2013

1.3   Current Malware Analysis Techniques are Limited

Unfortunately, the current techniques for malware analysis is far from being satisfactory. The current malware analysis techniques fall into two categories: static analysis and dynamic analysis. Common static analysis techniques, such as disassembler tools [7], can be easily defeated by various anti-analysis techniques, such as code packing [12], anti debugging [1], control-flow obfuscation [9], and others.

Dynamic analysis can cope with these anti-analysis techniques. Common dynamic analysis techniques, such as CWSandbox [15], NormanSandbox [3], and Anubis [2], run the malicious code in a special environment, such as a virtual machine or an emulator, and then observe its interaction with the environment by monitoring important system calls and API calls. However, they have many significant limitations:

• They cannot deal with kernel malware and dynamically generated code;
• They cannot monitor malware's behavior in a fine-grained manner (e.g., monitoring accesses to registers and memory);
• They cannot uncover hidden behaviors that only are exhibited under certain conditions;
• They cannot reason about the inner-working of malware.

Some research efforts [6, 11, 13, 14]) have been made to address some of these limitations, or to analyze specific kinds of malware. However, none of them can address the problem of malware analysis from a holistic view, and thus none of them can serve as a systematic and generic solution to the problem of automatic malware analysis.

1.4   Our Approach

At a high level, we take a *root-cause oriented approach* to the problem of automatic malware analysis. We aim to capture intrinsic natures of malicious behaviors, rather than external symptoms of existing attacks. Since the intrinsic natures stem deeply from malicious intents, detection and analysis techniques based on these intrinsic natures would be much more difficult to evade and thwart. Moreover, these techniques would be used to deal with entire classes of malicious behaviors effectively.

To realize this approach, we propose a new architecture for malware detection and analysis, called *whole-system out-of-the-box fine-grained dynamic binary analysis*. The basic idea to run an entire operating system (e.g., Windows) inside a whole-system emulator, and then run the binary code in this emulated environment. During execution of the binary code, we monitor and analyze its behaviors in a fine-grained manner (i.e., at instruction level), completely from outside (within the emulator). we propose a core technique, namely *layered annotative execution*, as a Swiss army knife, to fine-grained binary code analysis. Essentially, during the execution of each instruction in the emulated system, depending on the instruction semantics and the analysis purpose, we can annotate certain memory locations or CPU registers or update existing annotations. This is a layered approach, because we can place extra analysis process on top of the existing analysis to extract more insightful results. Based on an open-source whole system emulator, QEMU [4], we implement the new architecture and the core technique into a generic dynamic binary analysis platform, code-named *TEMU*, which will be detailed in Chapter 2.

On the basis of TEMU, we further propose a series of new techniques to analyze several different aspects of malicious behaviors, and implement these techniques in form of TEMU plugins. Specifically, we developed the following plugins:

- We developed *Renovo* [8] to capture intrinsic nature of code unpacking behavior for extracting unpacked code and data, which will be described in Chapter 3;
- We built *Panorama* [17] to characterize abnormal information access and processing behavior of privacy-breaching malware, which will be explained in Chapter 4;
- We developed *HookFinder* [16] to identify and understand malware's hooking behaviors, which will be presented in Chapter 5;
- We implemented *MineSweeper* [5] to uncover hidden behaviors and identify trigger conditions, which will be detailed in Chapter 6.

1.5 Our Contribution

In summary, we made the following contributions in this collection of work:

- A root-cause oriented approach to the problem of automatic malware detection and analysis.
- A new system architecture, called whole-system out-of-the box fine-grained dynamic binary analysis.
- A core technique, namely layered annotative execution for fine-grained dynamic binary analysis.
- A unified and extensible analysis platform, code-named TEMU, to realize the new architecture and the core technique.
- A series of new techniques for detecting and analyzing various aspects of malware.

References

1. Anti-debugger techniques. http://www.textfiles.com/virus/adebgtut.txt
2. Anubis: Analyzing unknown binaries. http://analysis.seclab.tuwien.ac.at/
3. ASA, N.: Norman Sandbox. http://sandbox.norman.no/ (2006)

4. Bellard, F.: QEMU, a fast and portable dynamic translator. In: USENIX 2005 Annual Technical Conference, FREENIX Track, pp. 41–46 (2005)
5. Brumley, D., Hartwig, C., Liang, Z., Newsome, J., Poosankam, P., Song, D., Yin, H.: Automatically identifying trigger-based behavior in malware. In: Book chapter in "Botnet Analysis and Defense", Editors Wenke Lee et. al. (2007)
6. Egele, M., Kruegel, C., Kirda, E., Yin, H., Song, D.: Dynamic spyware analysis. In: Proceedings of USENIX Annual Technical Conference (2007)
7. The IDA Pro Disassembler and Debugger. http://www.datarescue.com/idabase/
8. Kang, M.G., Poosankam, P., Yin, H.: Renovo: A hidden code extractor for packed executables. In: Proceedings of the 5th ACM Workshop on Recurring Malcode (WORM) (2007)
9. Linn, C., Debray, S.: Obfuscation of executable code to improve resistance to static disassembly. In: Proceedings of the 10th ACM Conference on Computer and Communications Security (CCS) (2003)
10. Annual worldwide economic damages from malware exceed 13 billion dollars. http://www.computereconomics.com/article.cfm?id=1225
11. Moser, A., Kruegel, C., Kirda, E.: Exploring multiple execution paths for malware analysis. In: Proceedings of the 2007 IEEE Symposium on Security and Privacy(Oakland'07) (2007)
12. the Ultimate Packer for eXecutables. http://upx.sourceforge.net/
13. Vasudevan, A., Yerraballi, R.: Cobra: Fine-grained malware analysis using stealth localized-executions. In: SP '06: Proceedings of the 2006 IEEE Symposium on Security and Privacy (S&P'06), pp. 264–279. IEEE Computer Society, Washington, DC, USA (2006). DOI http://dx.doi.org/10.1109/SP.2006.9
14. Wilhelm, J., cker Chiueh, T.: A forced sampled execution approach to kernel rootkit identification. In: Recent Advances in Intrusion Detection, pp. 219–235 (2007)
15. Willems, C.: CWSandbox: Automatic behaviour analysis of malware. http://www.cwsandbox.org/ (2006)
16. Yin, H., Liang, Z., Song, D.: HookFinder: Identifying and understanding malware hooking behavior. In: 15th Annual Network and Distributed System Security Symposium (2008)
17. Yin, H., Song, D., Egele, M., Kruegel, C., Kirda, E.: Panorama: Capturing system-wide information flow for malware detection and analysis. In: Proceedings of ACM Conference on Computer and Communication Security (2007)

Chapter 2
Dynamic Binary Analysis Platform

2.1 New Analysis Architecture

We propose a new architecture for dynamic binary analysis, called *whole-system out-of-the-box fine-grained dynamic binary analysis*. The basic idea to run an entire operating system (including common applications) inside a whole-system emulator, execute the binary code of interest in this emulated environment, and then observe and analyze the behaviors of this binary code from the emulator. This new architecture is motivated by the following considerations:

- **Dynamic analysis.** Malware is often equipped with various code obfuscation techniques, making pure static analysis extremely difficult. By actually executing the malware, dynamic analysis can overcome these code obfuscation techniques. This is because no matter what code obfuscation methods the malware is equipped with, as long as the malware exhibits the malicious behaviors during the dynamic analysis, we can observe and analyze these malicious behaviors.
- **Whole-system view.** A whole-system emulator presents us a whole-system view. The whole-system view enables us to analyze the operating system kernel and interactions between multiple processes. In contrast, many other binary analysis tools (e.g., Valgrind [17], DynamoRIO [4], Pin [13]) only provide a local view (i.e., a view of a single user-mode process). This is particularly important for analyzing malicious code, because many attacks involve multiple processes, and kernel attacks such as rootkits have become increasingly popular.
- **Out-of-the-box approach.** We perform analysis completely outside the execution environment. This out-of-the-box approach provides excellent isolation and good transparency. It is more difficult for malware to detect the presence of analysis environment and interfere with analysis results.
- **Fine-grained analysis.** Many analyses require fine-grained instrumentation (i.e., at instruction level) on binary code. By dynamically translating the emulated code, the whole-system emulator enables fine-grained instrumentation.

H. Yin and D. Song, *Automatic Malware Analysis: An Emulator Based Approach*, SpringerBriefs in Computer Science, DOI 10.1007/978-1-4614-5523-3_2, © The Author(s) 2013

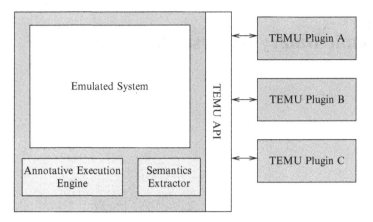

Fig. 2.1 Architecture of TEMU

We developed a system called TEMU to implement this new architecture. Figure 2.1 illustrates the architecture of TEMU. TEMU provides several key functionalities:

- **OS awareness.** The whole-system emulator only provides the hardware-level view of the emulated system, whereas we need a OS-level view to get meaningful analysis results. Therefore, we need a mechanism that can extract the OS-level semantics from the emulated system. For example, we need to know what process is currently running and what module an instruction comes from. To this end, we build the *semantics extractor* to extract OS-level semantics information from the emulated system.
- **Core analysis technique.** Many program analysis techniques require annotating data values according to semantics of each executed instruction. We propose a generic analysis technique, called layered annotative execution, and implement it in the *annotative execution engine*.
- **Plug-in architecture.** We need to provide a well-designed programming interface (i.e., API) for users to implement their own plugins on TEMU to perform their customized analysis. Such an interface can hide unnecessary details from users and reuse the common functionalities.

We implemented TEMU in Linux, based on an open-source whole-system emulator, QEMU [2]. At the time of writing, TEMU can be used to analyze binary code in Windows 2000, Windows XP, and Linux systems. Below we describe these three components respectively.

2.2 Semantics Extractor

The semantics extractor is responsible for extracting OS-level semantics information of the emulated system, including process, module, thread, symbol information, and function call context.

2.2.1 Process and Module Information

For the current instruction, we need to know which process, thread and module this instruction comes from. In some cases, instructions may be dynamically generated and executed on the heap.

Maintaining a mapping between addresses in memory and modules requires information from the guest operating system. We use two different approaches to extract process and module information for Windows and Linux.

For Windows, we have developed a kernel module called *module notifier*. We load this module into the guest operating system to collect the updated memory map information. The module notifier registers two callback routines. The first callback routine is invoked whenever a process is created or deleted. The second callback routine is called whenever a new module is loaded and gathers the address range in the virtual memory that the new module occupies. In addition, the module notifier obtains the value of the CR3 register for each process. As the CR3 register contains the physical address of the page table of the current process, it is different (and unique) for each process. All the information described above is passed on to TEMU through a predefined I/O port.

For Linux, we can directly read process and module information from outside, because we know the relevant kernel data structures, and the addresses of relevant symbols are also exported in the system.map file. In order to maintain the process and module information during execution, we hook several kernel functions, such as do_fork and do_exec.

2.2.2 Thread Information

For windows, we also obtain the current thread information to support analysis of multi-threaded applications and the OS kernel. It is fairly straightforward, because the data structure of the current thread is mapped into a well-known virtual address in Windows. In Linux, a thread is implemented as a light-weight process, appearing in the task linked list. So no extra handling is needed to obtain the thread information in Linux.

2.2.3 Symbol Information

Given a binary module, we also parse its header information in memory and extract the exported symbol names and offsets. After we determine the locations of all modules, we can determine the absolute address of each symbol by adding the base address of the module and its offset. This feature is very useful, because all windows APIs and kernel APIs are exported by their hosting modules. The symbol information conveys important semantics information, because from a function name, we are able to determine what purpose this function is used for, what input arguments it takes, and what output arguments and return value it generates. Moreover, the symbol information makes it more convenient to hook a function— instead of giving the actual address of a function, we can specify its module name and function name. Then TEMU will automatically map the actual address of the function for the user. In the current implementation, TEMU is able to parse memory images of PE and ELF binary modules.

2.2.4 Function Call Context

It is important, in many cases, to determine if some behavior executed in system or library code is actually performed on behalf of the program under analysis. In other words, we often need to tell if certain behavior is performed under the function call context of the program of interest.

We use the following observation to identify malicious behavior that is performed by trusted system modules on behalf of the malware: Whenever the malicious code calls a trusted function to conduct malicious behavior, the value of the stack pointer at the time of the function call must be greater than the value of the stack pointer at the time when the malicious behavior is actually performed. This is because one or more stack frames have to be pushed onto the stack when making function calls, and the stack grows toward smaller addresses on the x86 architecture.

Based on our observation, we use the following approach to identify the case when trusted code conducts malicious behavior on behalf of the code under analysis: Whenever the execution jumps into the code under analysis (or code derived from it), we record the current value of the stack pointer, together with the current thread identifier. When executing jumps out of this code, we check whether there is a recorded stack pointer for the current thread identifier, and if so, whether this value is smaller than the current stack pointer. If this is the case, we remove the record as the code is not on the stack anymore. Whenever an interesting behavior is observed, we check whether there is a recorded stack pointer under the current thread identifier. If so, we consider this behavior to be conducted by the code under analysis.

2.3 Annotative Execution Engine

We propose a generic technique for dynamic binary code analysis, namely *layered annotative execution*. During the execution of each instruction, depending on the instruction semantics, we can *annotate* the operands of this instruction or update the existing annotations.

We use a *shadow memory* to store and manage the annotations of each byte of the physical memory and CPU registers and flags. To support tracking memory being swapped in and out, we also have shadow memory for the hard disks. The shadow memory is organized in a page-table-like structure to ensure efficient memory usage.

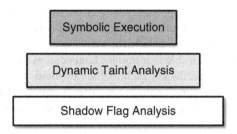

Fig. 2.2 A Layered Approach for Annotative Execution: One analysis technique is built on top of another to perform more advanced analysis. More concretely, "shadow flag analysis", "dynamic taint analysis", and "symbolic execution" are layered from bottom to top

With the shadow memory for the hard disks, the system can continue to track the annotations that have been swapped out.

We can perform annotative execution in a variety of ways. The most basic analysis is called *shadow flag analysis*, in which we may simply annotate certain memory locations or registers to be *dirty* or *clean*. A more advanced analysis is called *taint analysis*, in which we not only annotate certain memory locations and registers to be *tainted*, but also keep track of taint propagation. The most advanced analysis is called *symbolic execution*, in which we not only mark certain inputs (i.e, memory locations or registers) as tainted, but assign a meaningful symbol to these inputs. Then during taint propagation, we associate symbolic expressions to the tainted memory locations and registers. These symbolic expressions indicate how these variables are calculated from the symbolic inputs. Apparently, this is a layered approach: one analysis mechanism is built on top of another to perform more advanced analysis, as illustrated in Figure 2.2.

2.3.1 Shadow Flag Analysis

Shadow flag analysis is the most basic analysis in this layered architecture. Basically, depending on the execution context and the semantics of the current instruction, we determine to mark certain memory or register to be *dirty* or *clean*. Later, we can check the status of memory and registers, to determine which memory regions and registers are marked as dirty. To minimize the storage consumption of shadow memory, we only need to maintain the states of dirty memory regions and registers, and manage the states in a page-table-like structure.

2.3.2 Taint Analysis

Our dynamic taint analysis is similar in spirit to a number of previous systems [6, 8, 18, 21]. However, since our goal is to enable whole-system fine-grained taint analysis, our design and implementation is the most complete. For example, previous approaches either operate on a single process only [18, 21], or they cannot deal with memory swapping and disks [6, 8].

A TEMU plugin is responsible to introduce taint sources into the system. TEMU supports taint input from hardware, such as the keyboard, network interface, and hard disk. TEMU also supports tainting a high-level abstract data object (e.g. the output of a function call, or a data structure in a specific application or the OS kernel).

After a data source is tainted, we need to monitor each CPU instruction and DMA operation that manipulates this data in order to determine how the taint propagates. For data movement instructions and DMA operations, the destination will be tainted if and only if the source is tainted. For arithmetic instructions, the result will be tainted if and only if any byte of the operands is tainted. We also handle the following special situations.

Some instructions or instruction sequences always produce the same results, independent of the values of their operands. A good example is the instruction "xor eax, eax" that commonly appears in IA-32 programs as a compiler idiom. After executing this instruction, the value of eax is always zero, regardless of its original value. We recognize a number of such special cases and untaint the result.

A tainted input may be used as an index to access an entry of a table. The taint propagation policy above will not propagate taint to the destination, because the value that is actually read is untainted. Unfortunately, such table lookup operations appear frequently, such as for Unicode/ASCII conversion in Windows. Thus, we augment our propagation policy with the following rule: if any byte used to calculate the address of a memory locations is tainted, then, the result of a memory read using this address is tainted as well.

2.3.3 Symbolic Execution

Symbolic execution gives abstract interpretations of how certain values are processed on both data plane and control plane. On the data plane, symbolic execution allows registers and memory locations to contain symbolic expressions in addition to concrete values. Thus, a value in a register may be an expression such as X + Y where X and Y are symbolic variables. Consider a small program in Figure 2.3. After execution, we produce a symbolic expression for mem[10], which is mem[10] = y*3+5. This symbolic expression abstractly interprets how the content in this memory location is calculated from the relevant symbolic inputs on the data plane.

On the control plane, symbolic execution generates a path predicate, describing the constraints on the symbolic inputs need to satisfy for the program execution to go down that path. In the above example, the if statement $z < 10$ has to be true for the mem[10] to be assigned a new value. The symbolic execution can give us a path predicate y < 2, which abstractly describes what condition has to be satisfied in order to perform the assignment operation on L7.

When certain conditions are not satisfied, behaviors depending on these conditions will not be exhibited. In the above example, if the actual value of y is 3, then the if statement z<10 will not be true, and the operation on L7 will not be executed. To uncover the hidden behaviors, for each control flow decision that depends on symbolic inputs, we will determine which branches are feasible and try to explore all the feasible execution paths. More precisely, for each branch, we extract a symbolic expression as the path predicate, and use a theorem prover to determine if the path predicate can be *true*. In the above example, we will be able to explore both branches for the if statement on L6, because we determine the path predicate can be either *true* or *false*. Thus, we will be able to uncover the memory assignment on L7.

During symbolic execution, for each instruction, we need to determine if it should be executed symbolically. If so, we enqueue this instruction and its operands into the symbolic machine. In consequence, the instructions and states in the symbolic machine form a symbolic program. Then if we want to query the symbolic expression and path predicate of a symbol, we extract formulas from the symbolic program. In addition, whenever a control flow decision is dependent of a symbolic variable, we attempt to explore all feasible directions.

2.3.3.1 Generate Symbolic Program

An instruction can be executed concretely iff all operands of the instruction are concrete. Thus, deciding whether an instruction should be executed concretely or symbolically requires information about which data in the system is concrete and which is symbolic. Recall that the shadow memory associated with registers and memory indicates the status of each byte. A symbolic byte is marked as tainted. Thus, to determine if an instruction needs to be executed symbolically, we just need to check if any of its operands is tainted. If so, we perform symbolic execution, and mark the destination operand as tainted, just like normal taint propagation. Otherwise, we execute this instruction concretely.

Mixed execution means that many instructions will be executed concretely and never be executed on the symbolic machine. Therefore, if an instruction to be symbolically executed has any concrete operands, we must update those concrete values inside the symbolic machine.

Ideally, during symbolic execution, we would like to generate symbolic expressions and path predicates on the fly. However, this naive approach would incur unacceptable performance overhead at runtime. To optimize the performance, we perform "lazy symbolic execution". Its basic idea is to quickly perform as few operations as possible to guarantee fast runtime performance, and maintain the enough information for post analysis. Specifically, for each instruction that need to be executed symbolically, we enqueue that instruction, along with the relevant machine states (including all operands and other related memory and register states) into our symbolic machine. Then we quickly mark the destination operand

Fig. 2.3 A Simple Symbolic
Program

```
L1:  z = 10;
L2:  x = 2;
L3:  x = y*3;
L4:  z = x+4;
L5:  k = z+1;
L6:  if(z<10)
L7:     mem[10] = k;
```

as symbolic by checking the source operands. This strategy enables fast runtime performance. In consequence, the instructions and states in the symbolic machine form a symbolic program, just like the one in Figure 2.3.

2.3.3.2   Extract Symbolic Formulas

We take the following steps to extract a symbolic formula for a symbol from the symbolic program. First, we perform dynamic slicing on the symbolic program. This step removes the instructions that the symbol does not depend upon. After this step, the symbolic program will be reduced tremendously. Then we generate one expression by substituting intermediate symbols with their right-hand-side expressions. At last, we perform constant folding to further simplify the expression. Still use the program in Figure 2.3 as an example. To get the symbolic expression for mem[10], we perform dynamic slicing first. It would remove the instructions on L1 and L2. Then we perform symbol substitution, and we get a formula like below:

```
mem[10] = y*3+1+4
```

Then we perform constant folding on it, and finally get:

```
mem[10] = y*3+5
```

2.3.3.3   Explore Multiple Execution Paths

When executing a conditional jump instruction that depends on a symbolic condition, we attempt to explore all feasible paths. To determine if a path is feasible, we generate the path predicate for that path, and ask the Solver if this path predicate is satisfiable. The Solver is a theorem prover or decision procedure, which performs reasoning on symbolic formulas. TEMU is extensible; we can plug in any Solver appropriate, and our system thus can automatically benefit from any new progress on decision procedures, etc. Currently in our implementation, we use STP as the Solver [11, 12].

A satisfiable path predicate means a feasible path. We need to decide which feasible direction needs to be explored now. Thus, we need an algorithm to prioritize the paths in the malicious code. We may employ different heuristics to decide which path to pick from the set of feasible paths. For example, it can use breadth-first search, depth-first search, and other strategies. In our approach, our strategy is to explore as many conditional jumps which depend upon abstract symbols as possible. Thus, we take a BFS like approach.

Once we decide which direction to explore, we save the state of the emulated system, and then make the system execution go to that direction by changing the EIP register. Later, if we want to explore the other direction, we can simply restore the state and start execution from that point. More specifically, the saved state includes the states of whole emulated machine (such as registers, memory, and I/O devices), the state of shadow memory in TEMU, and the symbolic program. The size of this entire state can be large. We can employ various compression techniques to reduce the size. For example, we can save the relative state changes to an initial state, instead of the absolute state. Then we can perform common compression methods on the relative state to further reduce its size.

The functionality of state saving and restoring enables a distributed architecture for malware analysis. It may be still time-consuming to analyze a complex and big malware sample, in terms of the number of branches that depend upon symbolic inputs. A centralized controller may disseminate different saved states to multiple working nodes, such that they can explore multiple different execution paths in parallel. This architecture would significantly reduce the overall analysis time for a malware sample.

Moser *et al.* also build a malware analysis system that is capable of exploring multiple execution path [15]. In comparison, we independently propose and develop our system, as a more comprehensive solution to this problem. First, TEMU maintains path predicates with bit-level accuracy and can handle non-linear path constraints, whereas their system can only handle linear constraints. Second, their system saves and restores states for a specific process, assuming malware is only within one process, while our system handles whole-system states and thus can cope with malware that involves kernel code and multiple processes.

2.4 TEMU APIs

In order for users to make use of the functionalities provided by TEMU, we define a set of functions and callbacks. By using this interface, users can implement their own plugins and load them into TEMU at runtime to perform analysis. Currently, TEMU provides the following functionalities:

- Query and set the value of a memory cell or a CPU register.
- Query and set the taint information of memory or registers.
- Register a hook to a function at its entry and exit, and remove a hook. TEMU plugins can use this interface to monitor both user and kernel functions.
- Query OS-level semantics information, such as the current process, module, and thread.
- Save and load the emulated system state. This interface helps to switch between different machine states for more efficient analysis. For example, this interface

makes multiple path exploration more efficient, because we can save a state for a specific branch point and explore one path, and then load this state to explore the other path without restarting the program execution.

TEMU defines callbacks for various events, including (1) the entry and exit of a basic block; (2) the entry and exit of an instruction; (3) when taint is propagating; (4) when a memory is read or write; (5) when a register is read or written to; (6) hardware events such as network and disk inputs and outputs.

2.5 Related Work

Tools like DynamoRIO [4], Pin [13], Strata [20], and Valgrind [17] support fine-grained instrumentation of a user-level program. They all provide high-level interfaces to facilitate building custom analysis tools. However, as they can only instrument a single user-level process, they are not suitable to analyze the activities in the operating system kernel (e.g., kernel malware and kernel vulnerabilities) or applications that involve multiple processes. DynamoRIO, PIN and Strata are designed to achieve highly efficient dynamic instrumentation, whereas Valgrind is targeted at heavyweight analysis, such as shadow value analysis [16]. It eliminates the complexity of the x86 instruction set by first translating x86 instructions into intermediate representations, namely VEX statements. Like Valgrind, TEMU is designed to support myriad of in-depth analyses. It takes advantage of dynamic translation mechanism in QEMU to build more comprehensive analysis platform.

PinOS [5] is an extension to Pin for whole-system instrumentation. Hence, PinOS can be used to instrument both kernel and user-level code. To achieve whole-system instrumentation, PinOS is built on top of the Xen [1] virtual machine monitor with Intel VT technology. TEMU also enables whole-system instrumentation and offers a whole-system view. However, compared to PinOS, TEMU provides substantially better support, such as OS-level semantics extraction and layered annotative execution, for analysis tools built on top of it.

Dytan [7] is a platform for performing dynamic taint analysis. With the high-level interface provided by Dytan, custom taint analysis tools can be easily built. Dytan is based on Pin, and thus can only analyze a single user-level process. By contrast, TEMU is a whole-system analysis platform and provides even richer functionalities for various analysis purposes.

Nirvana [3] is another analysis platform for a user-level program, using software dynamic translation techniques. In particular, it is used to build a sophisticated instruction-level tracing and time-traveling debugging tool, called iDNA. A comprehensive tracing tool was also developed on top of TEMU. While Nirvana can only analyze a user-level program, TEMU can be used to analyze kernel code and multiple programs simultaneously, with extra functionalities, such as exploit detection, offline symbolic execution, etc.

Cobra [22] is a malware analysis platform. Cobra is implemented as a kernel module and inserted into the Windows kernel space to observe malware's execution in both user and kernel space. It uses a technique called localized execution to instrument and inspect malware's behavior. The localized execution technique is in spirit similar to dynamic translation techniques. Cobra takes an internal approach, because the analysis is performed in the same execution environment to be analyzed.

Ether [9] is another platform for malware analysis. Ether makes use of hardware virtualization techniques to observe malware's execution in a stealthy manner. Compared with Cobra, Ether takes an external approach. The analysis is performed outside the guest system, which in principle has better transparency than an internal approach. However, Ether is not an ideal platform for in-depth malware analysis, which requires instruction-level instrumentation. Although fine-grained instrumentation can be achieved through single-step mode, its significant performance overhead (hundreds of times slowdown) is unacceptable in many cases. In contrast, by using dynamic translation techniques, TEMU can perform in-depth malware with much better efficiency due to dynamic binary translation. However, emulation via dynamic translation is not as transparent as hardware virtualization [10, 14, 19]. We leave it as future work to build a more stealthy and efficient analysis platform by combining hardware virtualization and emulation techniques.

2.6 Summary

In this chapter, we presented a dynamic binary analysis platform, TEMU. In order to support a wide-spectrum of dynamic binary analysis needs, TEMU explores a unique design space. It is able to provide a whole-system view, perform out-of-the-box analysis, and bridge the semantic gap between hardware-level and OS-level views. To further facilitate fine-grained analysis, TEMU incorporates shadow flag analysis, taint analysis, and symbolic execution, and generalizes these techniques into a unified technique, layered annotative execution. This platform greatly simplifies the development of various malware analysis techniques, as we will demonstrate in the upcoming chapters.

References

1. Barham, P., Dragovic, B., Fraser, K., Hand, S., Harris, T., Ho, A., Neugebauer, R., Pratt, I., Warfield, A.: Xen and the art of virtualization. In: Proceedings of the 19th ACM Symposium on Operating Systems Principles (SOSP'03, pp. 164–177 (2003)
2. Bellard, F.: QEMU, a fast and portable dynamic translator. In: USENIX 2005 Annual Technical Conference, FREENIX Track, pp. 41–46 (2005)
3. Bhansali, S., Chen, W.K., de Jong, S., Edwards, A., Murray, R., Drinić, M., Mihočka, D., Chau, J.: Framework for instruction-level tracing and analysis of program executions. In: Proceedings of the 2nd International Conference on Virtual Execution Environments (VEE'06), pp. 154–163 (2006)

4. Bruening, D., Garnett, T., Amarasinghe, S.: An infrastructure for adaptive dynamic optimization. In: International Symposium on Code Generation and Optimization (CGO'03) (2003)
5. Bungale, P.P., Luk, C.K.: PinOS: A programmable framework for whole-system dynamic instrumentation. In: Proceedings of the 3rd international conference on Virtual Execution Environments (VEE'07), pp. 137–147 (2007)
6. Chow, J., Pfaff, B., Garfinkel, T., Christopher, K., Rosenblum, M.: Understanding data lifetime via whole system simulation. In: Proceedings of the 13th USENIX Security Symposium (Security'03) (2004)
7. Clause, J., Li, W., Orso, A.: Dytan: a generic dynamic taint analysis framework. In: Proceedings of the 2007 international symposium on Software testing and analysis (ISSTA'07), pp. 196–206 (2007)
8. Crandall, J.R., Chong, F.T.: Minos: Control data attack prevention orthogonal to memory model. In: Proceedings of the 37th International Symposium on Microarchitecture (MICRO'04) (2004)
9. Dinaburg, A., Royal, P., Sharif, M., Lee, W.: Ether: malware analysis via hardware virtualization extensions. In: Proceedings of the 15th ACM Conference on Computer and Communications Security, pp. 51–62 (2008)
10. Ferrie, P.: Attacks on virtual machine emulators. Symantec Security Response (2006)
11. Ganesh, V.: STP: A decision procedure for bitvectors and arrays. http://theory.stanford.edu/~vganesh/stp.html (2007)
12. Ganesh, V., Dill, D.L.: A decision procedure for bit-vectors and arrays. In: W. Damm, H. Hermanns (eds.) Computer Aided Verification (CAV '07), *Lecture Notes in Computer Science*, vol. 4590, pp. 524–536. Springer-Verlag, Berlin, Germany (2007)
13. Luk, C.K., Cohn, R., Muth, R., Patil, H., Klauser, A., Lowney, G., Wallace, S., Reddi, V.J., Hazelwood, K.: Pin: Building customized program analysis tools with dynamic instrumentation. In: Proc. of 2005 Programming Language Design and Implementation (PLDI) conference (2005)
14. Martignoni, L., Paleari, R., Roglia, G.F., Bruschi, D.: Testing cpu emulators. In: Proceedings of the 18th International Symposium on Software Testing and Analysis (ISSTA'09), pp. 261–272 (2009)
15. Moser, A., Kruegel, C., Kirda, E.: Exploring multiple execution paths for malware analysis. In: Proceedings of the 2007 IEEE Symposium on Security and Privacy(Oakland'07) (2007)
16. Nethercote, N., Seward, J.: How to shadow every byte of memory used by a program. In: Proceedings of the 3rd international conference on Virtual Execution Environments (VEE '07), pp. 65–74 (2007)
17. Nethercote, N., Seward, J.: Valgrind: a framework for heavyweight dynamic binary instrumentation. In: PLDI, pp. 89–100 (2007)
18. Newsome, J., Song, D.: Dynamic taint analysis for automatic detection, analysis, and signature generation of exploits on commodity software. In: Proceedings of the 12th Annual Network and Distributed System Security Symposium (NDSS) (2005)
19. Raffetseder, T., Krügel, C., Kirda, E.: Detecting system emulators. In: Information Security, 10th International Conference, ISC 2007, pp. 1–18 (2007)
20. Scott, K., Kumar, N., Velusamy, S., Childers, B., Davidson, J.W., Soffa, M.L.: Retargetable and reconfigurable software dynamic translation. In: Proceedings of the international symposium on Code generation and optimization (CGO'03), pp. 36–47. Washington, DC, USA (2003)
21. Suh, G.E., Lee, J.W., Zhang, D., Devadas, S.: Secure program execution via dynamic information flow tracking. In: Proceedings of the 11th International Conference on Architectural Support for Programming Languages and Operating Systems (ASPLOS'04) (2004)
22. Vasudevan, A., Yerraballi, R.: Cobra: Fine-grained malware analysis using stealth localized-executions. In: SP '06: Proceedings of the 2006 IEEE Symposium on Security and Privacy (S&P'06), pp. 264–279. IEEE Computer Society, Washington, DC, USA (2006). DOI http://dx.doi.org/10.1109/SP.2006.9

Chapter 3
Hidden Code Extraction

3.1 Background and Problem Scope

To thwart static malware analysis, malware writers usually have their programs heavily armored with various code obfuscation techniques. Such techniques include binary and source code obfuscation [4, 12], control-flow obfuscation [10], instruction virtualization [21], and binary code packing [18]. Here, we focus on identifying and extracting the hidden code generated using binary code packing, one of the most common code obfuscation methods. Code packing transforms a program into a packed program by compressing or encrypting the original code and data into packed data and associating it with a *restoration routine*. A restoration routine is a piece of code for recovering the original code and data as well as setting an execution context to the original code when the packed program is executed. Figure 3.1 illustrates how a packed program is executed. This technique is available as commercial products [3, 5, 16, 19, 20] and open-source tools. According to the anti-virus (AV) program test results of AV-Test GmbH [6], the detection rates of 8 major AV programs varied from 10% to 80% when known malware binaries have been packed.

Various tools have been developed to identify and extract the hidden code in packed executables. Commonly known tools such as PEiD [17] employ a simple pattern matching approach. These tools check an executable with a signature database to determine what kind of packing tool is used to create the executable. Then, using a priori knowledge about the packing tool, it is possible to extract the hidden binary from the executable [22]. Although this approach is usually fast and accurate for known packing tools, it is unable to detect novel and modified packing techniques. For example, a variant of the Bagle worm employed its own compression engine which is not known to the public [9]. In fact, by modifying the open source anti-reverse engineering tools like YodaProtector [23], it is easy for malware writers to implement new anti-reverse engineering algorithms and tricks.

Some tools attempt to solve this problem in a more generic way. Universal PE Unpacker [8] and PolyUnpack [18] make use of dynamic analysis to extract packed

H. Yin and D. Song, *Automatic Malware Analysis: An Emulator Based Approach*,
SpringerBriefs in Computer Science, DOI 10.1007/978-1-4614-5523-3_3,
© The Author(s) 2013

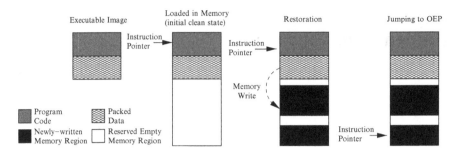

Fig. 3.1 How a Packed Program is Executed

binaries and find the OEP (i.e., Original Entry Point). They either rely on some heuristics or require disassembling the packed program. However, heuristics about packed code can fail in many cases and can be easily evaded. Correctly disassembling a binary program itself is challenging and error-prone, as demonstrated in [15]. To overcome the disassembly challenge required for packed code extraction, a tool like PolyUnpack needs to perform a series of static and dynamic analysis which leads to performance overhead and inaccuracy.

Problem Statement: Given an unknown binary program, we want to automatically detect if it exhibits code packing behavior, and if so, extract unpacked code and data from the packed program. We aim to capture the intrinsic nature of code unpacking behavior, which is independent of the packing techniques applied on the programs. By doing so, we can solve this problem in the most generic way, overcoming the limitations of previous approaches.

3.2   Approach Overview

We capture the following intrinsic nature of code unpacking behavior: no matter what packing methods or how many hidden layers are applied, the original program code and data should eventually be present in memory to be executed, and also the instruction pointer should jump to the OEP of the restored program code which has been written in memory at run-time. Taking advantage of this inevitable nature of packed executables, we propose a technique to dynamically extract the hidden original code and the OEP from the packed executable by examining whether the current instruction has been generated at run-time, after the program binary was loaded. For this purpose, we monitor if the instruction pointer jumps to the memory region which has been written after the program start-up. When a program is loaded in memory, we generate a memory map and initialize the map as *clean*. Whenever the program performs a memory write instruction, *e.g.,* mov %eax, [%edi] and push %eax, we mark the corresponding destination memory region as *dirty*, which means it is newly generated. Meanwhile, when the instruction pointer jumps

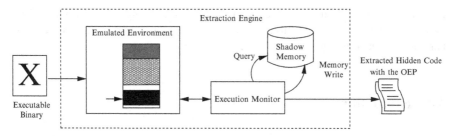

Fig. 3.2 Renovo Overview

to one of these newly-generated regions, we determine that there is a hidden layer hiding the original program code, and identify the newly-generated memory regions to contain the hidden code and data, and the address pointed by the instruction pointer as the original entry point (OEP). To handle the possible hidden layers that may appear later on, we initialize the memory map as clean again, after storing all the information extracted from the current hidden layer. Then, we repeat the same procedure until the time-out. Figure 3.2 illustrates the overview of this approach.

3.3 System Implementation

We implement Renovo, on top of TEMU, to automatically identify packed executables and extract their hidden code. Specifically, we make use of shadow flag analysis mechanism in layered annotative execution provided by TEMU. That is, Renovo observes the program execution in the emulated environment. Initially, the entire shadow memory is set as *clean*. In this case, the page table of the shadow memory is empty. During program execution, Renovo instruments memory writes within the observed process, and annotate the written memory regions as *dirty*. Meanwhile, it queries the shadow memory, and checks if any byte of the memory region that the current instruction occupies is dirty. If so, it can determine the instruction has been newly generated.

When checking newly generated instructions, we do not have to check every instruction. To optimize the performance, we check every basic block in the observed process. A basic block is a sequence of instructions with only one entry and one exit. Thus a basic block is a contiguous code region. At the block entry, we record its address. Then at the block exit, we check if there is any dirty memory locations within the region covering this block. If so, this block entry is the OEP, and we dump the pages containing dirty memory bytes.

In order to extract hidden code from packed executables with multiple hidden layers, we clean the dirty states in the shadow memory, and then repeat the extraction procedure. Note that determining whether a program has hidden code or not is an *undecidable* problem [18]. Thus, we introduce a configurable time-out parameter into the system. If we do not observe any hidden code being executed within this time-out, we terminate the extraction procedure. In the experiments, we set this parameter to be 4 minutes.

3.4   Evaluation

We describe two experiments and present the evaluation results, demonstrating that Renovo is an accurate and practical solution for extracting the original hidden code of packed executables.

3.4.1   Extracting from Synthetic Samples

To verify that Renovo generates accurate results, we have tested Renovo and two other extraction techniques, Universal PE Unpacker [8] and PolyUnpack [18], against the synthetic sample programs generated by using 14 different packing tools. These tools apply different packing techniques as well as encryption, code obfuscation, debugger detection, and instruction virtualization to thwart reverse engineering.

We use Microsoft notepad as an original binary to generate synthetic packed program samples. For all tools but Themida [21], the samples are created using the tools' default configuration. In the case of Themida, we generated two samples with slightly different configurations: one with instruction virtualization ("VM option") and one without it. Other than that, both options still use the same compression, encryption, and other techniques to protect the program from reverse engineering. We tested and ensured that none of these synthetic samples contains the binary string found in the .text section of the original notepad program. With the knowledge that these packing tools usually restore and execute the original binary instructions at run-time, we could verify the correctness of our extraction technique by comparing the extracted hidden code regions with the .text section of the original binary.

As shown in Table 3.1, Renovo fully extracted the original binaries processed by all but 3 packing tools, which are Armadillo, Obsidium, and Themida(w/ VM). But in the first two cases, the samples terminated before reaching the original program code, likely because the executables are not compatible with the Renovo's emulation engine. Nevertheless, Renovo still identified these two samples as packed executables because it successfully extracted hidden code and data from several initial hidden layers, which seem to be its restoration routines. In the case of a sample generated using Themida(w/ VM), Renovo extracted some hidden regions which do not match the original notepad binary. We believe this is the VM virtualization code equivalent to the original notepad instructions since we successfully extracted those from a sample generated using Themida(w/o VM).

Table 3.1 Extracting Hidden Code in Synthetic Samples

Tool	Size (KB)	Renovo		UUnP		PolyUnpack	
		result	time (sec)	result	time (sec)	result	time (sec)
None	68	no	N/A	no	N/A	no	N/A
Armadillo	564	error	44	error	1	part	1617
ASPack	53	yes	35	yes	3	part	181
ASProtect	153	yes	48	error	6	yes	62
FSG	46	yes	38	yes	3	yes	92
MEW	44	yes	36	yes	139	yes	739
MoleBox	108	yes	47	error	242	no	757
Morphine	72	yes	36	yes	1	yes	174
Obsidium	143	error	61	error	1	no	457
PECompact	49	yes	37	error	2	no	39
Themida(w/ VM)	1342	part	60	no	9	timeout	1800
Themida(w/o VM)	1067	yes	70	error	10	timeout	1800
UPX	47	yes	35	yes	3	yes	94
UPXS	47	yes	37	yes	4	yes	92
WinUPack	44	yes	38	error	12	part	33
YodaProtector	64	yes	36	error	1	part	62

Remark:

no	A tool identified a binary as not being packed.
yes	A tool extracted the whole original notepad binary.
part	A tool identified an incorrect entry point or could only extract parts of the original binary.
timeout	A tool did not terminate within the time-out period of 30 minutes.
error	A tool encountered errors or terminated prematurely.

Although UUnP requires *a priori* knowledge about the possible range of the OEP, it can run automatically without such input from a user. By default, it assumes that the OEP locates in the first program segmentation as identified by IDAPro and uses this contiguous memory segmentation as the possible range of the OEP. We ran UUnP using this default heuristic and found UUnP successfully extract the original notepad code from 6 out of 15 samples (Table 3.1). It failed on the sample generated by Themida(w/ VM) as the executable detected the presence of IDA's debugger. For the rest of the samples, UUnP encountered the exception handler routine and was unable to proceed to later execution steps. Nevertheless, note that UUnP is very efficient as it can extract most hidden code in less than 10 seconds.

We obtained the analysis results of PolyUnpack [18] by submitting samples to the Malfease website [13] of which PolyUnpack operates as its sub-module. We also asked the PolyUnpack authors to run our samples against a version of PolyUnpack that handles some forms of structured exception handling in addition to the functionalities presented on the Malfease website.

Table 3.2 Comparing
Renovo with Other
Unpackers on Real-world
Malware Samples

	Renovo	UUnP	PolyUnpack
Extracted results	366	186	171
IRC pattern found	363	176	86
Avg. time (sec.)	40.9	15.7	365.8

3.4.2 Extracting from Malware Samples

In this experiment, we test Renovo with the real malware samples which are protected by known and unknown packing techniques. We also used Universal PE Unpacker (UUnP) and PolyUnpack for comparison analysis like in the previous experiment.

To select the most-likely packed executables, we briefly examined the malware samples provided by Korea Information Security Agency (KISA) using PEiD [17]. From these samples, we collected 374 malware samples which are identified either to be packed by known tools like PECompact and UPX, or to contain *overlay* sections in their PE headers. (The samples with the overlay sections are likely to be packed executables.) According to the Norton Anti-Virus scan results, 7 of these samples are downloaders, and the rest are bot programs.

As shown in Table 3.2, Renovo identified most of the samples to be packed executables; only 8 out of total 374 samples were identified as normal executables. However, these 8 samples seem to have crashed or terminated before reaching the original hidden code. In comparison, both UUnP and PolyUnpack identified only about half of the samples to be packed executables. Like in the previous experiment, we also encountered exception handler problem when running UUnP on some of the samples. The average time for hidden code extraction is 40.9 seconds for Renovo, 15.7 seconds for UUnP, and 365.8 seconds for PolyUnpack. Considering that the system boot time of Renovo is about 30 seconds, the sheer code extraction time of Renovo is approximately 10 seconds which is less than that of UUnP. This is also a promising result when compared to the performance of Norton Anti-Virus. For the same set of malware samples, Norton Anti-Virus took 17 seconds per sample in average.

Unlike the evaluation using the synthetic samples where we have the original program binaries, it is difficult to verify the correctness of extracted code and data. Therefore, we examined extracted code and data to see if they contain any of the IRC commands that common bot programs use to communicate with control servers. Considering the fact that most of the samples (367 out of 374) are bot programs, the extracted code and data are likely to contain some of these IRC commands which are not present in the packed executables. As we see in the second row of Table 3.2, most of the extracted code and data extracted by Renovo contain these IRC command strings which have not been found in the packed malware samples.

Figure 3.3 shows the number of hidden layers found by Renovo and the number of corresponding samples. While most of the malware samples apply less than 20 hidden layers, some of the samples are found to use more than 500 hidden layers.

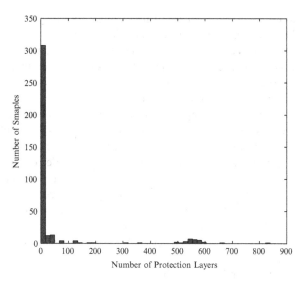

Fig. 3.3 Hidden Layers in Malware Samples

Most of these highly-layered samples are applying unknown packing techniques which are not in the PEiD signature list. We conjecture that they might be a new type of packing technique which generates and executes only some parts of the original code on the fly to protect itself from dynamic analysis techniques at run-time. We leave this for future research.

3.4.3   Performance Overhead

We measured the performance overhead of Renovo by running a sample program on both Renovo and normal environment. The sample program is a small test binary which outputs simple text messages and it was packed using the UPX packing tool. We found that the current version of Renovo shows a performance slowdown of 8 times on average compared to the normal execution environment. Considering that Renovo is aiming to provide hidden code extraction environment for malware analysis which usually takes several hours to days, this degree of slowdown in initial execution time is tolerable.

3.5   Related Work

Extracting and re-building the original program from a compressed or encrypted binary has been one of the major challenges for software reverse engineers and the security community. For known packing techniques, there exist corresponding unpackers [22]. However, given an arbitrary packed executable, which unpacker to use is still a problem. PEiD [17] is a tool for identifying compressed Windows PE binaries. Using the database of the signatures for known compression and encryption techniques, it identifies the packing method employed and, thus, suggests which unpacker can be applied. However, despite their ability to perfectly restore the original program, executables packed with unknown or modified methods are beyond the scope of this approach.

Universal PE Unpacker [8] and OllyBonE [1] are attempts to develop a comprehensive solution to this problem. As plug-in modules for IDA Pro [11] and Olly Debugger [2], both tools identify packed executables and their original entry points by using several heuristics. For example, Universal PE Unpacker assumes that GetProcAddress is always called to set up the import table after the original program is unpacked and before the program counter reaches the OEP. Also, it is not intended to be an automated unpacking tool because it must be given a priori knowledge about the the possible range of the OEP. OllyBonE sets the Break-on-Execution flag on the reserved memory sections used to accommodate unpacked code and data. When the CPU accesses these execution-protected pages, OllyBonE detects it and enables the extraction of the hidden code executed on OllyDbg. Although the OSes do not always enforce the assumptions where these heuristics work, in most of the cases, it produces correct results quickly. However, as shown in [18] and in our results, some malware can evade this heuristic based approach.

PolyUnpack [18] is a general approach for extracting the original hidden code without any heuristic assumptions. PolyUnpack takes advantage of the intrinsic nature of packed executables where the hidden code is generated and executed at run-time, and thus it is not present in the code section of the packed executable. As a pre-analysis step, PolyUnpack disassembles the packed executable to partition it into the code and data sections, Then it executes the binary instruction by instruction, checking whether the instruction sequence from the current point is in the code section identified in the pre-analysis step. The authors have implemented this approach and have shown that it can successfully identify and extract the hidden code in malware samples in the wild. However, in terms of performance, disassembling a program and single-step executing a binary significantly increase the computational complexity of its analysis.

Christodorescu et al. proposed several normalization techniques that transform obfuscated malware into a normalized form to help malware analysis [7]. Their unpacking normalization is similar to our approach. Its basic idea is to detect the execution of newly-generated code by monitoring memory writes after the program starts. We independently propose and implement our approach, and conduct more extensive experiments using various packed malware samples.

There has also been a commercial effort to enhance the detection rate against packed malware. McAfee applies the Generic Decryption Engine (GDE) technique to its antivirus products [14]. GDE analyzes the decryption (decompression) algorithm in the malware code and uses this algorithm to extract the hidden code before applying its detection engine. Ewido Networks employs an emulation-based technique to extract the hidden code of malware [9]. The details of how these mechanisms work are not present these papers, but some malware in the wild are still shown to be able to evade these commercial virus scanners [18].

3.6 Summary

To thwart reverse engineering, malware writers often try to hide their original programs by transforming them into packed executables. In this chapter, we propose a dynamic approach to extract the hidden code and data from these packed executable, and the contributions are three-fold:

First, we propose a fully dynamic method which monitors currently-executed instructions and memory writes at run-time. This approach maintains a shadow memory of the memory space of the analyzed program, observes the program execution, and determines if newly generated instructions are executed. Then it extracts the generated code and data. Assuming nothing about the binary compression and encryption techniques, we provide a means to extract the hidden code and information, which is robust against anti-reverse-engineering techniques.

Second, our approach provides additional information useful for further code analysis. Since it monitors the run-time memory writes at byte-level, we can extract the exact memory regions with newly-generated code and data. Moreover, even in the case that multiple hidden layers are applied to the binary, we can keep track of the restoration routines and extract information at each layer.

Finally, to demonstrate its effectiveness, we implement a system, Renovo. By evaluating it with synthetic samples and over 370 real-world malware samples, our experiments show that Renovo provides more accurate results than all previous approaches, and incurs acceptable performance overhead.

References

1. OllyBonE. http://www.joestewart.org/ollybone/
2. OllyDbg. http://www.ollydbg.de/
3. ASPack Software: ASPack and ASProtect. http://www.aspack.com/
4. Bhatkar, S., DuVarney, D.C., Sekar, R.: Address obfuscation: An efficient approach to combat a broad range of memory error exploits. In: Proceedings of the 12th USENIX Security Symposium (2003)
5. Bitsum Technologies: PECompact2. http://www.bitsum.com/pec2.asp
6. Brosch, T., Morgenstern, M.: Runtime packers: The hidden problem? https://www.blackhat.com/presentations/bh-usa-06/BH-US-06-Morgenstern.pdf (2006)
7. Christodorescu, M., Kinder, J., Jha, S., Katzenbeisser, S., Veith, H.: Malware normalization. Tech. Rep. 1539, University of Wisconsin, Madison, Wisconsin, USA (2005)
8. Data Rescue: Universal PE Unpacker plug-in. http://www.datarescue.com/idabase/unpack_pe
9. Graf, T.: Generic unpacking: How to handle modified or unknown PE compression engines. http://www.virusbtn.com/pdf/conference_slides/2005/Graf.pdf (2005)

10. Huang, Y.L., Ho, F.S., Tsai, H.Y., Kao, H.M.: A control flow obfuscation method to discourage malicious tampering of software codes. In: ASIACCS '06: Proceedings of the 2006 ACM Symposium on Information, computer and communications security, pp. 362–362. ACM Press, New York, NY, USA (2006). DOI http://doi.acm.org/10.1145/1128817.1128878
11. The IDA Pro Disassembler and Debugger. http://www.datarescue.com/idabase/
12. Linn, C., Debray, S.: Obfuscation of executable code to improve resistance to static disassembly. In: Proceedings of the 10th ACM Conference on Computer and Communications Security (CCS) (2003)
13. Project malfease. http://malfease.oarci.net/
14. McAfee: Advanced virus detection scan engine and DATs. http://www.mcafee.com/us/local_content/white_papers/wp_scan_engine.pdf
15. Nanda, S., Li, W., Lam, L., Chiueh, T.: BIRD: Binary interpretation using runtime disassembly. In: CGO '06: Proceedings of the International Symposium on Code Generation and Optimization, pp. 358–370. IEEE Computer Society, Washington, DC, USA (2006). DOI http://dx.doi.org/10.1109/CGO.2006.6
16. Obsidium Software: Obsidium. http://www.obsidium.de/show.php?home
17. PEiD. http://www.secretashell.com/codomain/peid/
18. Royal, P., Halpin, M., Dagon, D., Edmonds, R., Lee, W.: PolyUnpack: Automating the hidden-code extraction of unpack-executing malware. In: ACSAC '06: Proceedings of the 22nd Annual Computer Security Applications Conference on Annual Computer Security Applications Conference, pp. 289–300. IEEE Computer Society, Washington, DC, USA (2006). DOI http://dx.doi.org/10.1109/ACSAC.2006.38
19. Silicon Realms Toolworks: Armadillo. http://siliconrealms.com/index.shtml
20. Teggo: MoleBox Pro. http://www.molebox.com/download.shtml
21. Themida. http://www.oreans.com/
22. The Unpacker Archive. http://www.woodmann.com/crackz/Tools/Unpckarc.zip
23. Yoda Protector. http://sourceforge.net/projects/yodap/

Chapter 4
Privacy-breaching Behavior Analysis

4.1 Background and Problem Scope

Privacy-breaching malware, including spyware, keyloggers, network sniffers, stealth backdoors, and rootkits, collects users' private information, tampers with critical system states, and causes billions of dollars in damage. Surprisingly, even software provided by reputable vendors may contain code that performs undesirable actions which may violate users' privacy. For example, Google Desktop, a popular local file system search tool, actually sends sensitive user information such as the local search index files back to Google's servers in certain configuration settings [13]. In another widely publicized example, Sony Media Player installs a rootkit without the user's knowledge in order to enforce copyright restrictions and sends back users' music listening habits [21].

Malware detection and analysis is a challenging task, and current malware analysis and detection techniques often fall short and fail to detect many new, unknown malware samples. Current malware detection methods in general fall into two categories: signature-based detection and heuristics-based detection. The former cannot detect new malware or new variants. The latter are often based on some heuristics such as the monitoring of modifications to the registry and the insertion of hooks into certain library or system interfaces. Since these heuristics are not based on the fundamental characteristics of malware, they can incur high false positive and false negative rates.

We observe that numerous malware categories, including spyware, keyloggers, network sniffers, stealth backdoors, and rootkits, share similar fundamental characteristics, which lies in their malicious or suspicious information access and processing behavior. That is, they access, tamper, and (in some cases) leak sensitive information that was not intended for their consumption. For example, when a user inputs some text into an editor, benign software (except the editor) will not access this text, whereas a keylogger will obtain the text, and then send it to the attacker. This behavior is typically exhibited without the user's knowledge or consent and it is this fundamental trait that separates such malicious applications from benign software.

H. Yin and D. Song, *Automatic Malware Analysis: An Emulator Based Approach*,
SpringerBriefs in Computer Science, DOI 10.1007/978-1-4614-5523-3_4,
© The Author(s) 2013

Problem Statement: Given an unknown binary program, we want to automatically determine if this program exhibits malicious or suspicious information access and processing behavior and provide valuable insights about how the program accesses and processes the information in an abnormal way.

4.2 Approach Overview

At a higher level, our approach to automatically detect whether an unknown sample exhibits malicious behavior is a three-step process: test, monitor, and analyze. We focus on the analysis of Windows-based malware. Hence, we use an out-of-the-box installation of Microsoft Windows as the analysis environment. We regard all code that comes with this installation as being *trusted* (in contrast to the unknown sample about which we have no information). We load the sample to be analyzed into this environment and mark which files belong to the loaded sample. We then run the entire environment including Microsoft Windows and the loaded sample in our system. Figure 4.1 depicts the overview of this approach. The system consists of the taint engine, the test engine, the malware detection engine, and the malware analysis engine.

To perform our automatic malware detection and analysis, we run a series of automated tests, which is performed by the *test engine*. For each test, we generate events that introduce sensitive information into the guest system. This sensitive data is sent to some trusted application, and is not destined for the sample that is under analysis. We then monitor the behavior of the sample during the tests and record its information access and processing behavior with respect to the sensitive information introduced in the tests. To this end, we have designed the *taint engine*, which performs whole-system, fine-grained information flow tracking. It monitors how the sensitive information propagates within the whole guest system (including

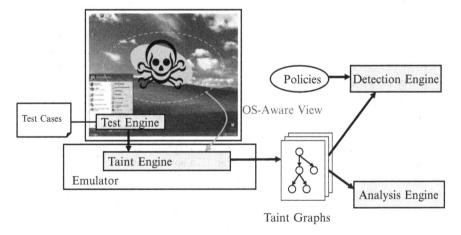

Fig. 4.1 Panorama System Overview

the propagation through the kernel and all applications). In particular, we need to investigate whether the information has propagated into the sample (i.e., whether it has been accessed by the sample) and what the sample has done with the information (e.g., sending it to an external server via the network). To monitor and record the information access and processing behavior of the sample, we make use of taint analysis technique in layered annotative execution.

Note that even though dynamic taint analysis has been proposed before, our approach is the first generic framework that applies dynamic taint analysis to the problem domain of detecting and analyzing privacy-breaching malware. Furthermore, our system offers several new capabilities that are necessary in our problem setting: (1) Our system is *OS-aware*—in addition to hardware-level taint tracking, we need to understand the high-level representations of hardware states for the analysis; (2) We also need to identify what actions are performed by or on behalf of the sample under analysis, even if the sample performs code unpacking and dynamic code generation, and executes actions through libraries, etc.; (3) Our monitoring needs to be whole-system and fine-grained, in order to precisely detect all actions of the sample.

The system-wide information behavior is captured by a graph representation, which we call *taint graph*. Taint graphs capture the taint propagation from the initial taint source (i.e., the sensitive information introduced in the tests) throughout the system. Using taint graphs, we can determine whether the unknown sample has performed malicious actions. In general, the decision whether an information access and processing behavior is considered malicious or benign is made with the help of policies. One characteristic property of many types of malicious code (such as keyloggers, spyware, stealth backdoors, and rootkits) is that they steal, leak or tamper with sensitive user information. Consider the following examples: (1) The user is typing input into an application such as a Microsoft Notepad, or is entering his user name and password into a web login form through a browser, while an unknown sample also accesses these keystrokes; (2) The user is visiting some websites, while an unknown sample accesses the webpages or URLs and sends them to a remote host; (3) The user is browsing a directory or searching a file, while an unknown sample intercepts the access to the directory entries and tampers with one or more entries. We devise a set of policies, which are used by the *malware detection engine* to detect malware from unknown samples. Finally, since taint graphs present invaluable insights about the samples' information access and processing behaviors, analysts can use the *malware analysis engine* to examine the taint graphs, for detailed analysis information.

4.3 System Design and Implementation

We designed and implemented a system, called *Panorama*, to explore the feasibility of our approach. Panorama is built as a TEMU plugin, and is composed of the following components: test engine, taint engine, malware detection engine, and malware analysis engine.

4.3.1   Test Engine

The test engine allows us to perform the analysis of samples and the detection of malicious code without human intervention. It executes a number of test cases that mimic common tasks that a user might perform, such as editing text in an editor, visiting several websites, and so on. To automatically run tests, the test engine is equipped with scripts that execute all steps necessary for each test case. For our current implementation, these scripts are based on the open source program AutoHotkey [1]. Scripts can be either manually written or automatically generated by recording user actions while a task is performed.

Whenever the test engine executes a certain test case, it introduces input (such as keystrokes or network packets) into the system. To determine which part of this input should be tainted (and with which taint label), the test engine cooperates with the taint engine. Currently, our system defines the following nine different types of taint sources: *text*, *password*, *HTTP*, *HTTPS*, *ICMP*, *FTP*, *document*, and *directory*, which will be discussed in Section 4.3.3. For example, when editing a document in an editor, the test engine asks the taint engine to send keystrokes to the editor, and label them as *text*; when entering password in a secure web form, the test engine asks the taint engine to send keystrokes and label them as *password*. When considering these cases, it becomes evident that the taint engine requires support from the test engine to properly label input. In both cases, the keystroke information enters the system. However, in the former case, the keystroke is considered *text* as it is sent to the one of the text editors. In the latter, the recipient of the input is a password field and the keystroke information is marked as *password*. Clearly, this information is test-specific and not available at the hardware level. The data received as a response to the web requests are tainted as *HTTP*. The packets received in response to ping requests are labeled *ICMP*. The information sent by the FTP server are marked *FTP*. Finally, when listing a directory, all accessed disk blocks that hold file directory information are tainted as *directory*. The communication between the test engine and the taint engine is via an intercepted registry writing API: the test engine writes information into a pre-determined registry entry, and taint engine intercepts this API call and then obtains the information.

4.3.2   Taint Engine

The taint engine performs whole-system OS-aware taint tracking, by utilizing the functionalities of semantics extractor and layered execution engine in TEMU. The system-wide propagation of tainted input introduced by the test engine forms a graph over the processes/program modules and OS resources. For example, assume that a keystroke is tainted as *text* because it is part of the input sent to a text editor. When a user process A reads the character that corresponds to the keystroke, this fact is recorded by linking the *text* taint source to process A. When this process later writes the character into a file F, from where it is then read by process B, we can establish a link from process A to the file, and subsequently from file F to process B. For clarity, we generate one graph for each taint source with a different label (that is, one graph that shows the flow of data labeled as *text*, one for *password*, . . .). For each taint source, the taint propagation originating from this source forms a directed graph. We call this graph a *taint graph*.

More formally, a taint graph can be represented as $g = (V, E)$, where V is a set of vertices and E is a set of directed edges connecting the vertices, and we use *g.root* to represent the root node of graph g (i.e., the taint source). A vertex can either represent an operating system object (such as a process or module), an OS resource (such as a file), or a taint source (such as keyboard or network input with the appropriate labels). An edge between two vertices v_1 and v_2 is introduced when tainted data is propagated from the entity that corresponds to v_1 to the entity that corresponds to v_2.

When generating the taint graphs, we map the hardware-level taint propagation information to operating-system level. For example, the taint engine determines which process and which module (such as which dll) has performed a certain operation, and it also keeps track of whether this operation is performed on behalf of the sample under analysis. Also, writes to disk blocks are attributed to file objects and network operations to specific network connections. To further simplify the taint graphs, we apply the following optimizations, without losing the dependencies between the sample under analysis and other objects: (1) we make the vertices for system kernel modules transparent; (2) for user-level instructions, if they are not derived from the sample under analysis (i.e., they are trusted), they are attributed to the processes they are running in, instead of the modules they are from.[1]

In a taint graph, each vertex is labeled with a (type, value) pair, where value is the unique name that identifies the vertex. For the root node, the type is one of the nine different input taint labels introduced previously. For any non-root node, the type represents the category of the node as a OS object, including process, module, keyboard, network, and file. Formally, the type of a vertex can be defined in a hierarchical form, as follows:

```
type ::= taint_source | os_object
taint_source ::= text | password |HTTP | HTTPS|
              FTP | ICMP | document | directory
os_object ::= process | module | network | file
```

Figure 4.2 shows an example of a taint graph. This graph reflects the procedure for Windows user authentication. While running in the background, a password thief catches the password and saves it to its log file "c:\ginalog.log". We use ellipses to represent process nodes and use shaded ellipses to represent the module node.

---

[1] In other words, the presence of a module node in a taint graph indicates at least one instruction of this module stems from the sample.

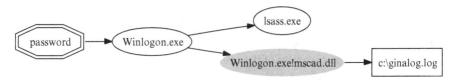

Fig. 4.2 An Example of Taint Graph

We use an octagon to represent the taint source (here, a password typed on the keyboard), and a rectangle to represent the other nodes.

4.3.3 Malware Detection Engine

Our essential observation is that numerous types of malicious code, including keyloggers, password thieves, network sniffers, stealth backdoors, spyware/adware, and rootkits, exhibit anomalous information access and processing behavior. Currently, we categorize three kinds of anomalous behavior: *anomalous information access*, *anomalous information leakage*, and *excessive information access*.

Anomalous information access behavior. For some information sources, a simple access performed by the samples under analysis is already suspicious. We refer to this behavior as *anomalous information access behavior*.

Considering the keyboard inputs, such information sources may include the text input sent to the text editor, the command sent to the command console, and the passwords sent to the Windows Logon dialog and secure web pages. Benign samples do not access these inputs, whereas *keyloggers* and *password thieves* will access these inputs. Keyloggers refer to the malicious programs that capture keystrokes destined for the other applications, and thus will access all these inputs. Password thieves, by definition, steal the password information, and therefore will access the password inputs. Note that password thieves can be a subset of keyloggers, because keyloggers may also record passwords.

Similarly, some network inputs are not supposed to be accessed by unknown samples. For example, ICMP is designed for network testing and diagnosis purpose, and hence only operating system and trusted utilities (e.g. ping.exe) use it. For many TCP and UDP applications, the incoming TCP and UDP traffic can only be accessed by their own and the operating system. Benign samples do not interfere with the process of these inputs. However, *network sniffers* and *stealth backdoors* access these inputs for different purposes. Network sniffers eavesdrop on the network traffic to obtain valuable information. Even though a network sniffer may not be directly interested in these inputs, it usually has to access them to check if they are valuable. Stealth backdoors refer to a class of malicious programs that contact with remote attackers without explicitly opening a port. To achieve stealthiness, the stealth backdoors either use an uncommon protocol such as ICMP,

Table 4.1 Test Cases and Introduced Inputs in Panorama

Test case description	Introduced inputs
1. Edit a text file and save it	text, document
2. Enter password in a GUI program	password
3. Log in a secure website	URL, password, HTTPS
4. Visit several websites	URL, HTTP
5. Log into an FTP server	text, password, FTP
6. Recursively list a directory	directory
7. Send UDP packets into the system	UDP
8. Ping a remote host	ICMP

create a raw socket, or intercept the network stack, in order to communicate with remote adversaries. The ICMP-based stealth backdoors will access ICMP traffic. The raw-socket-based stealth backdoor will access all the packets with the same protocol number. For example, a TCP raw socket will receive all TCP packets. The stealth backdoors intercepting the network stack will behave like a network sniffer.

Anomalous information leakage behavior. For some other information sources, it is acceptable for the samples to access them locally, but unacceptable to leak the information to third parties. For example, *spyware/adware* programs record users' surfing habits and send this private information to third parties. In contrast, benign BHOs (i.e., Browser Helper Objects) may access this information but will not send it out. We consider the following as information leakage: the sample under analysis accesses the information and then saves it to disk or sends it over the network. Note that saving the information to disk covers three situations: saving it to files, the registry, and even individual disk blocks. We consider information sources like HTTP, HTTPS, documents, and URLs fall into this category.

Excessive information access behavior. For some information sources, benign samples may access some of them occasionally, while malicious samples will access them excessively to achieve their malicious intent. We refer to it as anomalous information excessive access behavior.

The directory information is such a case. *Rootkits* exhibit excessive access behavior to the directory information, because they attempt to conceal their presence in the filesystem by intercepting the accesses to directory information and removing the entries that point to their files. Thus, when recursively listing directories, we will see the rootkit samples accessing many disk blocks that contain directory information. A benign program may access some directory entries, or even scan directories occasionally. However, it is very unlikely that it accesses the same directories at the same time while we list directories.

Test cases and policies. According to the above discussion, we compile the following test cases and introduce the inputs with corresponding labels, as shown in Table 4.1. Specifically, we introduce *text, password, URL* inputs from the keyboard, *HTTP, HTTPS, FTP, ICMP,* and *UDP* inputs from the network, and *document* and *directory* input from the disk. Note that in the test case 6, to eliminate the possibility that a benign program scans the same directory at a different time, we clean the taint labels of the visited directory entries after finishing with listing the directory. After finishing all the test cases, the test engine waits for a while (a configurable parameter) and then shuts down the guest machine.

From the above discussion, we specify the following policies: (1) *text, password, FTP, UDP* and *ICMP* inputs cannot be accessed by the samples; (2) *URL, HTTP, HTTPS* and *document* inputs cannot be leaked by the samples; (3) *directory* inputs cannot be accessed excessively by the samples. More formally, we show how these policies are enforced on the taint graphs:

$$\forall g \in G, (\exists v \in g.V, v.type = \texttt{module}) \wedge$$
$$g.root.type \in \{\texttt{text}, \texttt{password}, \texttt{FTP}, \texttt{UDP}, \texttt{ICMP}\}$$
$$\rightarrow Violate(v, \text{``No Access''}) \tag{4.1}$$

$$\exists g \in G, (\exists v \in g.V, v.type = \texttt{module}) \wedge$$
$$(g.root.type \in \{\texttt{URL}, \texttt{HTTP}, \texttt{HTTPS}, \texttt{document}\}) \wedge$$
$$(\exists u \in descendants(v), u.type \in \{\texttt{file}, \texttt{network}\})$$
$$\rightarrow Violate(v, \text{``No Leakage!''}); \tag{4.2}$$

$$(\forall g \in G, g.root.type = \texttt{directory} \rightarrow$$
$$\exists v \in g.V, v.type = \texttt{module})$$
$$\rightarrow Violate(v, \text{``No Excessive Access''}) \tag{4.3}$$

In addition to manually specifying the policies, it is possible to automatically generate policies by using machine learning techniques. First, we can gather a representative collection of malware and benign samples as our training set. Using this training set, Panorama will extract the corresponding taint graphs. Then, we need to develop a mechanism to transform a taint graph into a feature vector. Based on the feature vectors for the benign and malicious samples, standard classification algorithms can be applied to determine a model. Using this model, novel samples can then be classified. We will further explore this approach in our future work.

4.3.4 Malware Analysis Engine

Given a taint graph, the first step is to check this graph for the presence of a node that corresponds to the sample under analysis. If such a node is present, we obtain the information that the sample has accessed certain tainted input data. This is already suspicious, because the test cases are designed such that input data is sent to trusted applications, but never to the sample under analysis. Once we determine that a sample has accessed certain input, the sample's successor nodes in the graph can be examined. This indicates what has been done with the data that was captured. Such insights can be instrumental for system administrators and analysts to understand the behavior and actions of malware.

As an example, recall the taint graph previously shown in Figure 4.2. This taint graph has been produced by automatically analyzing the behavior of the password thief program GINA spy [11]. Note that the entered password is received by the Windows Logon process (`Winlogon.exe`). This process passes the password on to `lsass.exe` for subsequent authentication. Interestingly, the password data is also accessed by the sample under analysis (`mscad.dll`), which is loaded by `Winlogon.exe`. This code module reads the password and saves it to a file called `c:\ginalog.log`. The graph correctly reflects how the user password is processed by Windows, and how the password thief intercepts it.

4.4   Evaluation

Our evaluation consisted of three parts. First, we investigated the effectiveness of our taint-graph-based malware detection approach using a large body of real-world malware and benign samples. Then, by using Google Desktop as a case study (i.e., a sample from a vendor whose privacy policy we believed we could trust), we explored the amount of detailed information that we could extract from the taint graph of an unknown sample. Third, we performed tests to evaluate the performance overhead of our prototype. In all our experiments, we ran Panorama on a Linux machine with a dual-core 3.2 GHz Pentium 4 CPU and 2GB RAM. On top of Panorama, we installed Windows XP Professional with 512M of allocated RAM.

4.4.1   Malware Detection

Our malware collection consisted of 42 real-world malware samples, including 5 keyloggers, 2 password thieves, 2 network sniffer, 3 stealth backdoors, and 22 spyware BHOs, and 8 rootkits. Some of these samples were publicly available on the Internet (e.g., from web sites such as *www.rootkit.com*), while others were collected from academic researchers and an Austrian anti-virus company. Furthermore, we downloaded 56 benign, freely-available samples from a reputable and trustworthy web site (*www.download.com*). These benign samples were freeware programs from a wide range of different application domains (such as browser plug-ins, system utilities, and office productivity applications), with the size up to 3MB.

To further facilitate the experiments, we developed a tool using Python to run the samples and automatically perform the installation procedure (if required) using

Table 4.2 Detection Results on Malware and Benign Samples using Panorama

Category	Total	False Negatives	False Positives
Keyloggers	5	0	-
Password thieves	2	0	-
Network sniffers	2	0	-
Stealth backdoors	3	0	-
Spyware/adware	22	0	-
Rootkits	8	0	-
Browser plugins	16	-	1
Multi-media	9	-	0
Security	10	-	2
System utilities	9	-	0
Office productivity	4	-	0
Games	4	-	0
Others	4	-	0
Sum	98	0	3

several heuristics. The tool can handle 70% of the samples in our test set. For the remaining samples, some required manual configuration (they were all malware samples), and the others were not properly handled by the heuristics. We then manually installed the remaining samples. We installed up to 3 samples each time. After that, we ran the test cases. We set the test engine to wait for 5 minutes before shutting down the guest machine. Depending on the installation delay, the whole procedure lasts 15 to 25 minutes.

Table 4.2 summarizes the results of this experiment. We can see that Panorama was able to correctly identify all malware samples, but falsely declared three benign samples to be malicious.

Two of these false positives were personal firewall programs. The third false positive was a browser accelerator. By checking the taint graphs related to these three samples, we observed that the information access and processing behaviors of these benign samples closely resemble that of malware. In fact, the two personal firewalls install packet filters and monitor all network traffic. Hence, their behavior resembles that of a malicious network sniffer. In the case of the browser accelerator, we observed that the application prefetches web pages on behalf of the browser and stores them into its own cache files. This behavior resembles that of spyware that monitors the web pages that a user is surfing. The reason for our false positives is that our taint-graph-based detection approach can only identify the information access and processing behavior of a given sample, but not its intent. In real-life, the taint graphs are invaluable for human analysts, as they help them to quickly determine and understand whether an unknown sample is indeed malicious, or whether it is benign software that is exhibiting malware-like behavior.

4.4.2 Malware Analysis

In order to determine how well we are able to perform detailed analysis on an unknown sample, we chose Google Desktop for a case study. This application claims in its privacy policy [14] that it will index and store data files, mail, chat logs, and the web history of a user while the user is working on her system. Furthermore, if the special configuration setting "Search Across Computers" is enabled, Google Desktop will securely transmit copies of the user's index files to Google servers. Hence, Google Desktop, in fact, exhibits some malware-like behavior, as the index files may contain sensitive information about a user (e.g., a list of web sites that the user has visited), and these files are sent to an external server.

First, we downloaded the installation file (*GoogleDesktopSetup.exe*). Before installing the tool, we marked the installation file such that we could track which components would be installed into the system. After the installation was complete, we observed that 18 executables and shared libraries, as well as a dozen data files were installed.

Second, we ran the test cases, using the default settings of Google Desktop (in which "Search Across Computers" is disabled). After performing the test cases, we observed that some components extracted from the installation file accessed the tainted inputs, including HTTPS, HTTP and document. All of this information was later saved into the index files in the local installation directory. To determine if the information is sent out to remote hosts, we kept the system alive for 12 hours. However, we did not observe this behavior.

Third, we changed the settings of Google Desktop and enabled the feature "Search Across Computers". Then, we ran the test cases again and kept the system alive for another 30 minutes. It was evident from the generated taint graphs that, in this mode, Google Desktop did leak the collected information via HTTPS connections to Google servers. We picked a representative taint graph, which clearly illustrates how the components of Google Desktop process the incoming traffic of an HTTP connection from the QEMU web site we visited, (see Figure 4.3).

By examining this taint graph, we can draw several conclusions: (1) the incoming web page was first received and processed by the Internet Explorer (IEXPLORE.EXE), which later saved the content into a cache file (qemu[1].htm) under the temporary Internet file folder; (2) a component from Google Desktop (GoogleDesktopAPI2.dll) was loaded into the IEXPLORE.EXE, obtained the web page, and passed it over to a stand-alone program also from Google Desktop (GoogleDesktopIndex.exe); (3) GoogleDesktopIndex.exe further processed this information and saved it into two data files (rpm1m.cf1 and fiih.ht1) in its local installation directory; and (4) it sent some information derived from the web page to a remote Google server (72.14.219.147) through an HTTPS connection.

With the capability provided by Panorama, we could confirm that Google Desktop really sends some sensitive information if a special feature is activated (as it also claims in its privacy policy).

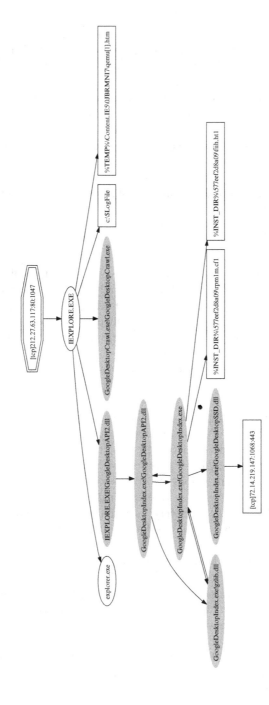

Fig. 4.3 A Taint Graph for Google Desktop

4.4.3   Performance Overhead

We measured Panorama's performance overhead using several utilities in Cygwin, such as *curl*, *scp*, *gzip*, and *bzip2*. When running these tools, we tainted file and network inputs accordingly. We found that the current un-optimized implementation of Panorama suffers a slowdown of 20 times on average.

4.5   Related Work

Malware detection approaches Signature based malware detection has been in use for years to scan files on disk and even memory for known signatures. Although semantic-aware signature checking [7] improves its resilience to polymorphic and metamorphic variants, the inherent limitation of the signature based approach is its incapability of detecting previously unseen malware instances. Its usefulness is also limited by the rootkits that hide files on disk and, as demonstrated in Shadow Walker [5], may even hide malware footprints in memory.

Behavior based malware detection identifies malicious programs by observing their behaviors and system states (i.e., detection points). By recognizing deviations from "normal" system states and behaviors, behavior based detection may identify entire classes of malware, including previously unseen instances. There are a variety of detections that examine different detection points. Strider GateKeeper [24] checks auto-start extensibility points in the registry to determine surreptitious restart-surviving behaviors. VICE [4] and System Virginity Verifier [20] search for various hooks that are usually used by rootkits and the other malware. Behavior based detection can be defeated, either by exploring stealthier methods to evade the known detection points, or by providing misleading information to cheat detection tools. In addition, current detection tools usually reside together with malicious programs, and therefore expose to complete subversion. In contrast, our system overcomes these three weaknesses. First, it captures the characteristic information access and processing behavior of malware, and thus cannot be easily evaded. Second, it detects malware based on the hardware-level knowledge and makes very few assumption at software level, and hence cannot be easily cheated. Third, it is implemented completely outside of the victim system, and so strongly protected from being subverted.

The cross-view based rootkit detection technique (e.g. Blacklight [3], Rootkit Revealer [19], and Strider Ghostbuster [2]) identifies hidden files, processes, registry entries by comparing two views of the system: the upper-level view is derived from calling common APIs, while the low-level view is obtained from system states in the kernel or from hardware if applicable. In comparison, our approach for rootkit detection has two advantages: (1) the cross-view based technique requires enumerating all files and registry entries, etc. to find hidden entries, which often takes several hours, whereas our approach only takes a few minutes; (2) the result given by the cross-view based technique can only identify a list of hidden entries, while our approach recognizes the rootkit directly.

Dynamic Taint Analysis Dynamic taint analysis has been applied to solve and analyze other security related problems. Many systems [8, 9, 17, 18, 22] detect exploits by tracking the data from untrusted sources such as the network being misused to alter the control flow. Chow et al. made use of whole-system dynamic taint analysis to analyze how sensitive data are handled in operating systems and large programs [6]. The major analysis was conducted in Linux, with source code support of the kernel and the applications. Egele et al. also utilized whole-system dynamic taint analysis to examine BHO-based spyware behavior [10]. Vogt et al. extended the JavaScript engine with dynamic taint analysis to prevent cross-site scripting attacks [23]. Our system is independently developed with OS-aware analysis for closed-source operating systems, and devises a unified machinery for detecting malware from several different categories.

Information flow analysis Our system works by analyzing taint graphs to identify suspicious information access and processing behavior of foreign code. This is related to previous work that performs forensic analysis based on information flows. For example, some systems track the flow of information between operating system processes to perform intrusion analysis [16], intrusion recovery [12], and malware removal [15]. However, these systems typically monitor the system call interface and thus, are not as comprehensive and do not provide the same level of precision as our technique. Another limitation of previous systems is that it is often not possible to precisely track data while it is processed by a program. This can introduce incorrect connections between data objects or lead to missed information flows. Also, previous systems do not apply to kernel-mode attacks. Thus, we believe that by performing whole-system, fine grained information flow tracking, our method provides higher accuracy than previous work, and we can also handle kernel attacks.

4.6 Summary

In this chapter, we have proposed *whole-system fine-grained taint analysis* to discern fine-grained information access and processing behavior of a piece of unknown code. This behavior captures the intrinsic characteristics of a wide-spectrum of malware, including keyloggers, password sniffers, packet sniffers, stealth backdoors, BHO-based spyware, and rootkits. Thus, the detection and analysis relying on it cannot be easily evaded. To evaluate the effectiveness of this approach, we have designed and developed a system, called Panorama. In the experiments, we have evaluated 42 malware samples and 56 benign samples. Panorama yields zero false negative and very few false positives. Then we use Google Desktop as a case study. We have demonstrated that Panorama can accurately capture its information access and processing behavior, and we confirm that it does send back sensitive information to remote servers. We believe that a system such as Panorama will offer indispensable assistance to malware analysts and enable them to quickly comprehend the behavior and inner-workings of malware.

References

1. AutoHotkey. http://www.autohotkey.com/
2. Beck, D., Vo, B., Verbowski, C.: Detecting stealth software with strider ghostbuster. In: Proceedings of the 2005 International Conference on Dependable Systems and Networks (DSN'05), pp. 368–377 (2005)
3. Blacklight. http://www.europe.f-secure.com/exclude/blacklight/
4. Butler, J., Hoglund, G.: VICE–catch the hookers! In: Black Hat USA (2004). http://www.blackhat.com/presentations/bh-usa-04/bh-us-04-butler/bh-us-04-butler.pdf
5. Butler, J., Sparks, S.: Shadow walker: Rasing the bar for windows rootkit detection. In: Phrack 63 (2005)
6. Chow, J., Pfaff, B., Garfinkel, T., Christopher, K., Rosenblum, M.: Understanding data lifetime via whole system simulation. In: Proceedings of the 13th USENIX Security Symposium (Security'03) (2004)
7. Christodorescu, M., Jha, S., Seshia, S., Song, D., Bryant, R.: Semantics-aware malware detection. In: Proceedings of the 2005 IEEE Security and Privacy Conference (2005)
8. Cost, M., Crowcroft, J., Castro, M., Rowstron, A., Zhou, L., Zhang, L., Barham, P.: Vigilante: End-to-end containment of internet worms. In: 20th ACM Symposium on Operating System Principles (SOSP 2005) (2005)
9. Crandall, J.R., Chong, F.T.: Minos: Control data attack prevention orthogonal to memory model. In: Proceedings of the 37th International Symposium on Microarchitecture (MICRO'04) (2004)
10. Egele, M., Kruegel, C., Kirda, E., Yin, H., Song, D.: Dynamic Spyware Analysis. In: Proceedings of the 2007 Usenix Annual Conference (Usenix'07) (2007)
11. GINA spy. http://www.codeproject.com/useritems/GINA_SPY.Asp
12. Goel, A., Po, K., Farhadi, K., Li, Z., de Lara, E.: The taser intrusion recovery system. In: Proceedings of the 20th ACM Symposium on Operating Systems Principles(SOSP'05) (2005)
13. Google's desktop search red flag. http://www.internetnews.com/xSP/article.php/3584131
14. Google Desktop - Privacy Policy. http://desktop.google.com/en/privacypolicy.html
15. Hsu, F., Chen, H., Ristenpart, T., Li, J., Su, Z.: Back to the future: A framework for automatic malware removal and system repair. In: Proceedings of the 22nd Annual Computer Security Applications Conference (ACSAC'06) (2006)
16. King, S.T., Chen, P.M.: Backtracking intrusions. In: Proceedings of the 19th ACM Symposium on Operating Systems Principles (SOSP'03), pp. 223–236 (2003)
17. Newsome, J., Song, D.: Dynamic taint analysis for automatic detection, analysis, and signature generation of exploits on commodity software. In: Proceedings of the 12th Annual Network and Distributed System Security Symposium (NDSS) (2005)
18. Portokalidis, G., Slowinska, A., Bos, H.: Argos: an emulator for fingerprinting zero-day attacks. In: EuroSys 2006 (2006)
19. Rootkit revealer. http://www.sysinternals.com/Files/RootkitRevealer.zip
20. Rutkowska, J.: System virginity verifier: Defining the roadmap for malware detection on windows systems. In: Hack In The Box Security Conference (2005). http://www.invisiblethings.org/papers/hitb05_virginity_verifier.ppt
21. Sony's DRM Rootkit: The Real Story. http://www.schneier.com/blog/archives/2005/11/sonys_drm_rootk.html
22. Suh, G.E., Lee, J.W., Zhang, D., Devadas, S.: Secure program execution via dynamic information flow tracking. In: Proceedings of the 11th International Conference on Architectural Support for Programming Languages and Operating Systems (ASPLOS'04) (2004)

23. Vogt, P., Nentwich, F., Jovanovic, N., Kirda, E., Kruegel, C., Vigna, G.: Cross-Site Scripting Prevention with Dynamic Data Tainting and Static Analysis. In: Proceeding of the Network and Distributed System Security Symposium (NDSS'07) (2007)
24. Wang, Y.M., Roussev, R., Verbowski, C., Johnson, A., Wu, M.W., Huang, Y., Kuo, S.Y.: Gatekeeper: Monitoring Auto-Start Extensibility Points (ASEPs) for spyware management. In: Proceedings of the Large Installation System Administration Conference (LISA'04) (2004)

Chapter 5
Hooking Behavior Analysis

5.1 Background of Hooking Attacks

One important malware attacking vector that need to be thoroughly understood is its hooking mechanism. Malicious programs implant hooks for many different purposes. Spyware may implant hooks to get notified of the arrival of new sensitive data. For example, keyloggers may install hooks to intercept users' keystrokes; password thieves may install hooks to get notified of the input of users' passwords; network sniffers may install hooks to eavesdrop on incoming network traffic; and BHO-based adware may also install hooks to capture URLs and other sensitive information from incoming web pages. In addition, rootkits may implant hooks to intercept and tamper with critical system information to conceal their presence in the system. Malware with a stealth backdoor may also place hooks on the network stack to establish a stealthy communication channel with remote attackers.

Several tools [2, 10, 13] detect hooking behaviors by checking known memory regions for suspicious entries. However, they need prior knowledge of how existing malware implants hooks. Therefore, they become futile when malware uses new hooking mechanisms. This concern is not hypothetical. Recently, new stealthy kernel backdoors [14, 17] are reported to employ a novel hooking mechanism for intercepting the network stack. All existing detection methods have failed to detect this type of malware.

5.2 Problem Statement

Given a malware sample, we aim to determine whether it contains hooking behaviors. A hooking behavior can be formalized as follows. A malicious program C attempts to change a memory location L of the operating system, to implant a *hook H*. When a certain event happens, the operating system will load the hook H, and then starts to execute malicious code F in program C. We refer to the address of F as *hook entry*, and L as *hook site*.

H. Yin and D. Song, *Automatic Malware Analysis: An Emulator Based Approach*,
SpringerBriefs in Computer Science, DOI 10.1007/978-1-4614-5523-3_5,
© The Author(s) 2013

Fig. 5.1 An SSDT Hooking
Example

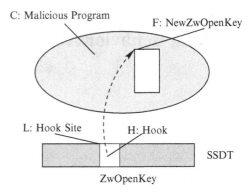

```
#define SYSTEMSERVICE(_function) \
  KeServiceDescriptorTable.ServiceTableBase \
  [*(PULONG)((PUCHAR)_function+1)]
void HookSyscalls() {
  ...
  OldZwOpenKey = SYSTEMSERVICE(ZwOpenKey);
  SYSTEMSERVICE(ZwOpenKey) = NewZwOpenKey;
  ...
}
```

The above code snippet shows a piece of pseudo code that hooks an entry in the System Service Descriptor Table (SSDT) of Windows system. This hooking mechanism is used in many kernel-mode malware samples, such as the Sony Rootkit [15]. In this example, the hook entry F is NewZwOpenKey, and the hook site L is the entry for ZwOpenKey in the service descriptor table, and the hook H is the address of NewZwOpenKey, as illustrated in Figure 5.1.

If we detect hooking behaviors in a malware sample, we want to provide some valuable insights about hooking mechanism, in form of a graphical representation, *hook graph*. A hook graph tells us two main characteristics of a hooking mechanism: *hook type* and *implanting mechanism*.

Hook Type Depending how it is interpreted by the CPU, a hook H can be either a *data hook* or a *code hook*. A data hook is interpreted as data by the CPU, and is used as the destination address of some control transfer instruction to jump into the hook entry F. For example, the hook in Figure 5.1 is a data hook, because it is the address of the hook entry, and is interpreted as the jump target. A code hook is interpreted as code by the CPU. A code hook contains a jump-like instruction (such as jmp and call), and is injected to overwrite some system code (such as kernel modules and common DLLs). When a code hook is activated, the execution is redirected into the malicious code F. We need to detect hooking behaviors in both cases, and we should be able to tell what kind of hook it is when we detect one. As we will see later, the policies used to detect hooking behaviors are different between these two categories due to their different nature.

Implanting Mechanism Malware has two choices to install H into L. First, it may directly write H into L using its own code. Second, it may call a function to achieve it on its behalf. Windows system provides several APIs for applications to register various event handlers (i.e., hooks). For example, `SetWindowsHookEx` allows an application to register a hook for certain Windows event, such as keystroke events. Whenever a keystroke is entered into the system, Windows will call the hook function provided by this application. In addition, functions like `memcpy` and `WriteProcessMemory` can overwrite a memory region on behalf of their callers. Thus, once we identify a hook, we need to determine which method the malware used to register the hook.

If the malware directly modifies L to install H, we need to understand where L is, and how the malware sample obtains L. Since L is usually not located in a fixed place, malware has to find it from some static point. This static point can be a global system symbol, or the result of a function call. After obtaining this static point, malware may walk through the data structures referenced by it to eventually locate L. The example in Figure 5.1 makes use of this method, and the hook site L is calculated from a global symbol `KeServiceDescriptorTable`. For this type of implanting mechanism, the hook graph answers the following questions:

- Where is the static point?
- How does the malware obtain the static point?
- How does it infer the final location L from the static point?

If the malware invokes an external function to register H, we need to identify the function's address and name. In addition, we need to know the actual arguments that are used to call this function. The function call and its argument list can give semantic information about how the hook and what kind of hook is registered. For example, if we identify that a malicious program calls `SetWindowsHookEx` to register a hook, we are able to tell from the first argument what type of hook is registered. For this type of implanting mechanism, the hook graph answers the following questions:

- What is the external function, including its entry address and its name?
- What arguments does the malware use to invoke this function?

5.3 Our Technique

We make the following key observation. Malicious code makes changes, including memory and the other machine state changes, to the execution environment as it runs. We call these changes *impacts*. Obviously, a hook H is one of the impacts made by the malicious code, and this impact finally redirects the execution control flow into the malicious code. Hence, if we are able to identify all the impacts of the malicious code, and observe one of the impacts being used to cause the execution to be redirected into the malicious code, we can determine a hook installed by the malicious code. Furthermore, we are also interested in how an impact is formulated, for the purpose of understanding hooking mechanism. Therefore, we identify *initial impacts*, the newly introduced impacts by the malicious code, and then keep track of the impacts propagating over the system.

Based on this key observation, we propose *fine-grained impact analysis* for hook detection, and *semantics-aware impact dependency analysis* for hook analysis.

Hook Detection: Fine-grained Impact Analysis We mark all the initial impacts made by the malicious code at byte level. The initial impacts include data written directly by the malicious code, and data written by the external code (through function calls) on its behalf. Then we keep track of the impacts propagating through the whole system. During the execution, if we observe that the instruction pointer (i.e., EIP in x86 CPUs) is loaded with a marked impact, and the execution jumps immediately into the malicious code, then we identify a hook. Furthermore, in this case, we have determined that the jump target is the hook entry F, the memory location that the instruction pointer is loaded from is the hook site L, and the content within L is the hook H.

Hooking Mechanism Analysis: Semantics-aware Impact Dependency Analysis Once identifying a hook H, we want to understand the hooking mechanism. During the impact propagation, we record into a trace the details about how the impacts are propagated in the system. Therefore, from the trace entry corresponding to the detected hook H, we can perform backward dependency analysis on the trace. The result gives how the hook H is formulated and installed into the hook site L. However, such a result is difficult to understand, because it only provides hardware-level information and sometimes can be enormous. We combine OS-level semantics information with the result, and perform several optimizations to hide unnecessary details. The final output is a succinct and intuitive graphical representation, assisting malware analysts to understand its hooking mechanism.

Note that our approach would catch "normal" hooking behaviors. Windows provides a number of APIs, such as CreateThread and CreateWindow, for applications to register their callback functions. Windows will invoke these callbacks on certain events. These function calls that register normal hooks can be compiled into a white-list. Then if one of these normal hooks is captured by our detection step, we can classify it as normal, by extracting its hooking mechanism and comparing it with the white-list. In practice, we find this white-listing approach very effective. Note that "normal" hooks are not considered false positives in our case, since our goal is to extract and analyze any hooking mechanism which may be employed by the sample of interest.

5.4 System Design and Implementation

To demonstrate the feasibility of our approach, we design and implement a system, *HookFinder*, to identify the hooking behavior and understand the hooking mechanism.

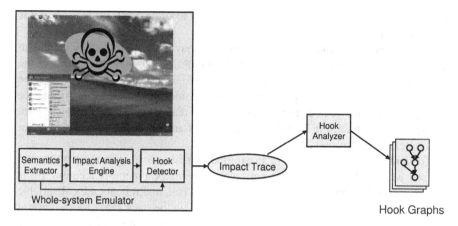

Fig. 5.2 HookFinder System Overview

As illustrated in Figure 5.2. HookFinder is built as a plugin of our dynamic binary analysis platform, TEMU. The malware to be analyzed is executed in the emulated Windows guest system. HookFinder consists of two components: *hook detector* and *hook analyzer*. The hook detector performs fine-grained impact analysis and detects hooks. To analyze hooking mechanisms, the impact propagation events, as well as necessary OS-level semantics information, are recorded into a trace, called the *impact trace*. Note that TEMU provides OS-level semantics information of the emulated execution environment. The *hook analyzer* analyzes the impact trace and generates a succinct and intuitive graphical representation, *hook graph*. The hook graph conveys essential information for malware analysts to easily understand the hooking mechanism.

5.4.1 Hook Detector

The hook detector performs fine-grained impact analysis. More specifically, the hook detector marks initial impacts made by the malicious code, keeps track of impact propagation, and detect diverted control flow caused by impacts.

Mark initial impacts. We need to identify all the initial impacts that can be used to install hooks. This is important, because if we fail to mark some initial impacts, malware writers may exploit this fact to evade our detection.

First, we consider that an instruction from malicious code directly makes an impact. When an executable binary is loaded into the system, a module space is allocated for it, and the code and data segments from the binary are copied into this module space and initialized. Note that the semantics extractor in TEMU is able to tell which module space belongs to the sample under analysis. Then, for an instruction located in that module, we need to mark its impact accordingly. That is, we mark the destination operand, either a memory location or a CPU register, if it is not marked already.

In addition, we consider that malicious code may make an impact by calling an external function. For example, it may call ReadFile to obtain the address of the hook entry F from a configuration file, and then install it as the hook H into the hook site L by calling memcpy. If we do not consider this situation, H will not be marked. Therefore, we need to mark the output of that external function too. Again, the semantics extractor in TEMU is able to tell if an instruction is executed under the context of an external function call.

To identify the impacts made in an external function, we treat memory writes and register writes differently. For memory writes, we mark a memory location if it is written under the context of the external function call, and it is not a local variable on the stack. To determine a local variable, we obtain the stack range for the current thread from the semantics extractor, and compare the memory location with the value of ESP on the entry of the external function call: if the memory location is smaller than the value of ESP and within the stack range, then it is a local variable. For register writes, we only need to consider EAX. According to the function calling conventions (i.e., _cdecl and _stdcall) in Windows, EAX contains the return value when applicable, while the other general-purpose registers (except the stack pointer ESP) remain unchanged. Now we need to determine if EAX contains the return value and mark it accordingly. We save the value of EAX on the entry of an external function call, and then on the exit of the function, check if EAX is changed. If so, we mark this EAX.

Furthermore, malware may dynamically generate new code. Since self-generated code is also part of impacts made by the malicious code, the memory region occupied by it must have already been marked. Thus, we can determine if an instruction is generated from the original malicious binary by simply checking if the memory region occupied by that instruction is marked. If so, we also treat that code region as malicious code, and mark the inputs taken by the self-generated code too.

Track impact propagation. The hook detector keeps track of the impacts propagating throughout the system. It tracks data dependencies between source and destination operands. That is, if any byte of any source operand is marked, the destination operand is also marked. In addition, for a memory source operand, if its address becomes marked, it also marks the destination operand. This policy enables us to track how the malicious code walks through a data structure, starting from a marked pointer to the data structure. The hook detector utilizes the taint analysis technique in layered annotative execution provided by TEMU to track impact propagation. Note that the hook detector keeps track of impacts propagating over the whole system, including the disk. It still keeps track of the impacts that are swapped out to disk, or written to the registry and filesystem. Therefore, it is able to detect the hooks that are registered through the registry and filesystem.

Here, impact analysis is slightly different from traditional taint analysis, in the way how it deals with immediate operands. That is, if an instruction has an immediate operand, impact analysis checks if the memory region occupied by this immediate is marked and if so, propagates the impact accordingly. In contrast, traditional taint analysis systems treat immediate operands as clean. In our scenario, the malicious code may overwrite the system code with manipulated immediate numbers in the instructions. For example, in the code hook case, the malicious code may inject into the system code a jump instruction with a hard-coded target address, to redirect the execution to the malicious code. This immediate operand is a crucial impact that is deliberately injected by the malicious code to set up a hook. Therefore, we need to check immediate operands.

To enable subsequent hook analysis, the hook detector performs an extra operation during the impact propagation. That is, we assign a unique identifier to each marked byte of the destination operand. We refer to this identifier as *dependency ID*. Then for each instruction that creates or propagates the marked data, we write a record into the impact trace. The record contains the relationships between the dependency IDs of marked source and the destination operand, associated with other detailed information about that instruction.

Detect hooks. The hook detector detects a hook by checking if the control flow is affected by some marked value, which redirects the execution into the malicious code. More precisely, we observe whether the instruction pointer EIP is marked, and the execution jumps immediately from the system code into the malicious code region, or the code region generated from the malicious code. If the conditions are satisfied, we identify a hook: the jump target is the hook entry F, the memory location that EIP is loaded from is L, and the content in L is H.

The above policy functions properly for identifying data hooks, but is problematic for code hooks. This is because a code hook is a piece of code generated by the malicious code, and thus is treated as malicious code by the above policy. Therefore when the code hook redirects the execution to the malicious code, the above policy will not raise an alarm because it sees the execution being transferred from malicious code to malicious code. To solve this problem, we extend the above policy such that the execution transitions from a code hook region into malicious code will raise an alert.

Then the question is how to distinguish code hook regions with other self-generated code regions. Self-generated code usually remains in the module space of the malicious code, or stays in a region that is not occupied by any module (such as in heap), whereas a code hook region is a piece of code that overwrites a code region in a different module. Therefore, during execution, if the currently executed basic block is marked and from a different module, and EIP is marked and jumps into the malicious code, we identify it as a code hook.

5.4.2 Hook Analyzer

Once a suspicious hook is identified, the hook analyzer is able to extract essential information about its hooking mechanism by performing *semantics-aware dependency analysis* on the impact trace. The procedure consists of the following three steps: (1) from the hook H, perform backward dependency analysis on the impact trace, and generate hardware-level hook graph; (2) with the OS-level semantics information, transform the hardware-level hook graph into an OS-level hook graph; and (3) if necessary, simplify the hook graph by hiding unnecessary details and merging similar nodes. We detail these steps respectively.

Hardware-level Hook Graph. A hook graph represents dependencies among malware's instructions that are used to implant a hook. A node of a hook graph corresponds to an instruction involving hooking behavior; an edge of a hook graph points from an instruction setting an operand to an instruction using the operand as source.

Recall that each record in the impact trace has dependency information. With the hook H identified by our hook detector, we create the first node in our hook graph, representing the instruction that activates H. We then obtain the hook's dependency ID ID_h, and locate the record that defines ID_h in the impact trace. Finally, we search backwards in the impact trace to add dependency information. Specifically, for each record R in the impact trace, if it creates a new dependency ID id that is used in the hook graph, we added a node N representing the instruction corresponding R, and add edges from N to other nodes that uses id as source operands in their corresponding instructions. We perform this backward search recursively until we reach the beginning of the trace. Besides the dependency information, each record contains detailed information about an instruction, such as its address and the values of its operands. If the instruction is executed under the context of an external function, the record also contains the entry address of that external function, and the value of ESP on the entry of call. We also put these details into the corresponding nodes. The resultant graph is the hardware-level hook graph.

Figure 5.3 shows a hardware-level hook graph built from a hook in Sony Rootkit [15], which employs the same hooking mechanism as the sample shown in Figure 5.1. A rectangle node denotes an instruction propagating malware's impacts. A diamond node denotes that its successor's destination address is affected by the malware's impacts. Note that to save space, we only display really important information for each node, such as the instruction address and the disassembled instruction. For each memory operand, we show its address and value. If the instruction is executed under the context of an external function call, we also show the entry of the function call and the ESP value on the entry.

OS-level Hook Graph. With the OS-level semantics information provided by the semantics extractor, we can transform a hardware-level hook graph into an OS-level hook graph. Given the address of an instruction, we can show which module it belongs to and its offset to the module base. Similarly for memory access, we can determine if it falls into any module space. If the memory access is to a symbol, we can even resolve its symbol name. Given the entry address of an external function, we can resolve its function name. Then, the resulting graph is an OS-level hook graph. Figure 5.4 illustrates the OS-level hook graph transformed from Figure 5.3. We can see that Figure 5.4 correctly reflects the hook registration procedure shown in Figure 5.1. That is, symbols ZwOpenKey and

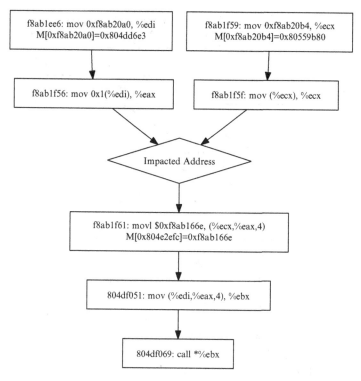

Fig. 5.3 Hardware=level Hook Graph for Sony Rootkit

KeServiceDescriptorTable are used to calculate the hook site *L* (shown in the diamond-shaped node), and an address (aries.sys+66e) is written into *L*. This is the hook *H*, the address of the hook entry *F*.

In addition to resolving function names, HookFinder also extracts function arguments from an impact trace. Since pushing arguments onto the stack is also part of the impacts made by a malware sample, the information about these arguments is already recorded in the impact trace. To extract a function's arguments, HookFinder locates the first record *R* of the activation of the function. The records preceding *R* contain function arguments, but may also contain other non-argument impacts made by the malware. As the impacts trace has information about the value of register ESP at the beginning of the function's activation, we only include the impacts within a certain distance to the value of ESP. In the current implementation, we search for up to 10 four-byte words following the location of ESP as arguments.

Graph Simplification. A hook graph can be very complex in some cases. For better readability and clarity, we simplify it using the following criteria: (1) if two adjacent nodes belong to the same external function call, we merge them into a single virtual node; (2) if two adjacent nodes are direct-copy instructions, such as mov, push, and pop, we merge them into a single node, because these instructions propagate

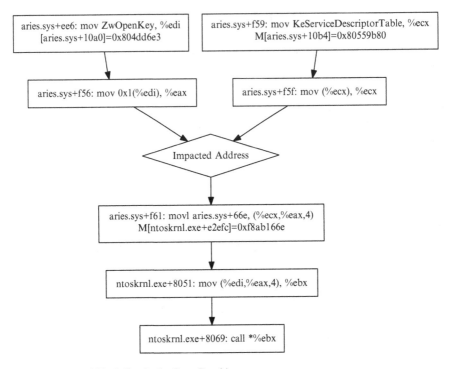

Fig. 5.4 OS-level Hook Graphs for Sony Rootkit

the same value without modification. We apply these two criteria repeatedly on our hook graph until no nodes can be merged. The result is often a graph much clearer to be interpreted.

5.5 Evaluation

We evaluated HookFinder with eight malware samples. In Table 5.1, we characterize these samples according to whether they are packed, whether they are kernel or user threats, and which categories they belong to.

5.5.1 Summarized Result

In the experiment, HookFinder has successfully identified hooks for all the samples. We summarize the results in Table 5.2. In the second column of Table 5.2, we list the elapsed time for each sample. It breaks down into two parts: the runtime for running the sample in the emulated environment (shown as the first number), and

Table 5.1 Malware Samples Analyzed in HookFinder

Sample	Size	Packed?	Kernel/User	Category
Troj/Keylogg-LF	64KB	Y	User	Keylogger
Troj/Thief	334KB	N	User	Password Thief
AFXRootkit [1]	24KB	Y	User	Rootkit
CFSD [4]	28KB	N	Kernel	Rootkit
Sony Rootkit [15]	5.6KB	N	Kernel	Rootkit
Vanquish [18]	110KB	N	User	Rootkit
Hacker Defender [9]	96KB	N	Both	Rootkit
Uay Backdoor [17]	212KB	N	Kernel	Backdoor

the runtime for generating hook graphs (as the second number). After executing a sample, we wait for 2-3 minutes to make sure it has fully started. In order to trigger potential hook behavior, we then perform a series of simple interactions with the emulated system, including listing a directory, and pinging a remote host, which may cost another 2 or 3 minutes. The runtime for generating hook graphs varies from 2 seconds to 33 minutes, depending on the trace size, the number of hooks, and other factors. In total, HookFinder spends up to 39 minutes on a sample during the evaluation, which is efficient compared to manual malware analysis that can last hours or days.

The third column lists the size of the impact trace for each sample. As we can see, the maximum size in the table is 14G, which is acceptable for a complex program executing millions of instructions.

The fourth and fifth column shows the number of suspicious hooks and the total number of identified hooks, for each sample. We found some normal hooks registered by the following functions: *EVENT_SINK_AddRef, FltDoCompletePro-cessingWhenSafe, StartServiceDispatcherA, CreateThread, CreateRemoteThread,* and *PsCreateSystemThread*. Note that our approach does not distinguish the intent of a hooking behavior. Thus, we will identify all hooks in the first place; then we check normal hooks by comparing them with our white-list.

The last column gives essential information about the hooking mechanism. We found that three samples installed code hooks. All three samples derive the hook sites by calling *GetProcAddress*. Vanquish directly writes the hooks into the hook sites, whereas AFXRootkit and Hacker Defender call *WriteProcessMemory* and *NtWriteVirtualMemory* respectively to achieve it. The other six samples installed data hooks, four of which call external functions to install the hooks. In particular, CFSD calls *FltRegisterFilter*, and Trojan/Keylogg-LF and Troj/Thief call *SetWindowsHookEx*. We also extracted arguments for these function calls, and we found that Trojan/Keylogg-LF installed a WH_KEYBOARD_LL hook, and Trojan/Thief installed a WH_CALLWINDPROC hook. The remaining two samples directly write hooks into hook sites. The static points are *KeServiceDescriptorTable* and *NdisRegisterProtocol* for Sony Rootkit and Uay Backdoor, respectively.

Table 5.2 Summarized Experimental Results using HookFinder

Sample	Runtime	Trace	Hooks		Hooking Mechanism
			Total	Mal	
Troj/Keylogg-LF	6m+9m	3.7G	2	1	Data, Call:SetWindowsHookEx(WH.KEYBOARD.LL,...)
Troj/Thief	4m+3s	143M	1	1	Data, Call:SetWindowsHookEx(WH.CALLWINDPROC,...)
AFXRootkit	6m+33m	14G	4	3	Code, Call:writeProcessMemory
CFSD	4m+2m	2.8G	5	4	Data, Call:FltRegisterFilter
Sony Rootkit	4m+2s	25M	4	4	Data, Direct, Static Point:KeServiceDescriptorTable
Vanquish	6m+12m	4.4G	11	11	Code, Direct, Static Point:GetProcAddress
Hacker Defender	5m+27m	7.4G	4	1	Code, Call:NtWriteVirtualMemory
Uay backdoor	4m+25s	117M	5	2	Data, Direct, Static Point:NdisRegisterProtocol

5.5.2 Detailed Result for Uay backdoor

HookFinder identified five data hooks in total for this sample. We reviewed the generated hook graphs, and we found that three of them were installed by *PsCreateSystemThread*. This kernel function creates a system thread with the thread entry provided by the caller. Thus, these three hooks are normal hooks. The other two are suspicious, and their hook graphs are similar. We show one graph in Figure 5.5.

As we can see in Figure 5.5, there are two branches in the bottom. The left branch describes how the hook site L was inferred, and the right branch presents how the hook H was formulated. From the top of the right branch, we can see that H originated from the output of a function call *NdisAllocateMemoryWithTag*. This kernel function is used to allocate a memory region in the kernel space. According to the function's semantics, this output has to be the address of the allocated memory region. This address is finally implanted into the hook site L.

From the top of the left branch, we observe that L is derived from the output of a function call *NdisRegisterProtocol*. This kernel function registers a network protocol. According to the function semantics, we believe this output is the protocol handle in the second argument. This handler points to an internal data structure maintained by the Windows kernel. Then we can see the instruction (at uay.sys+1695) reads a field with the offset 0x10 in this data structure. The obtained value (v_1) is then used as a pointer to read another value (v_2) from the offset 0x10 in the data structure pointed by v_1, in the subsequent instruction (at uay.sys+16a0). Then, the instruction (at uay.sys+1589) adds v_2 with 0x40, and the resulted value is eventually used as the hook site L. We believe that this sample actually walks into this internal data structure that it obtains from *NdisRegisterProtocol*, and locates the designated hook site L. Interestingly, the definition of the data structure for the protocol handle created from *NdisRegisterProtocol* is not released in any documentation from Microsoft, but this malware sample seems to be able to understand this data structure, and knows how to locate the desired hook site from it.

The hook graph for another suspicious hook is very similar to this one, except that it adds v_2 with 0x10. With the knowledge of how this internal structure is defined, we would be able to tell which two functions this malware sample actually hooked.

By analyzing this sample using HookFinder, we are able to unveil a novel mechanism for intercepting the network stack employed by malware. That is, malware can tamper with the function pointers in some kernel data structures associated with registered network protocols. With this important understanding, we can verify and protect the integrity of these data structures, to defend against this kind of hooking mechanism.

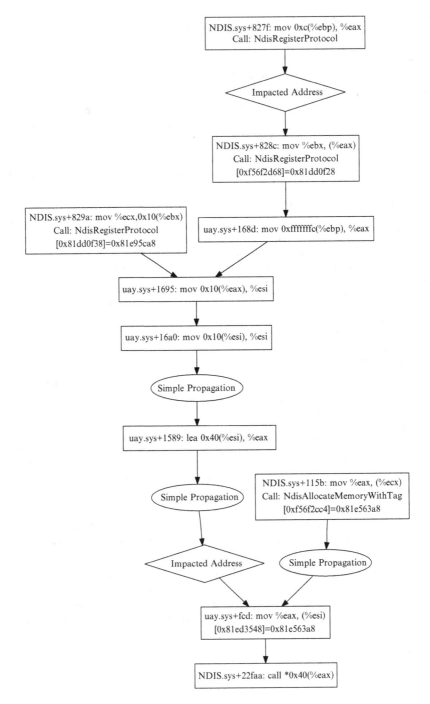

Fig. 5.5 Hook Graph for Uay

5.6 Related Work

Hook Detection Researchers have developed several tools, such as VICE [2], System Virginity Verifier [13], and IceSword [10], to detect the existence of hooks in the system. With prior knowledge how malicious code usually set hooks, these tools examine known memory regions for suspicious entries. The common examined places are system service descriptor table (i.e., SSDT) exported by the OS kernel, interrupt descriptor table (i.e., IDT) that stores interrupt handlers, import address tables (i.e., IAT) and export address tables (i.e., EAT) of important system modules. Assuming that important system modules do not modify their code (with a few exceptions), System Virginity Verifier checks if code sections of important system DLLs and drivers remain the same in memory as those in the corresponding binaries on disk. In nature, these tools fall into misuse detection, and thus cannot detect hooks in previously unknown memory regions. In comparison, our approach captures the intrinsic characteristics of hooking behaviors: one of the malware's impacts has to be used to redirect the system execution into the malicious code. Therefore, it can identify unknown hooking behaviors. Moreover, it also provides insights about the hooking mechanisms.

Dynamic Taint Analysis The fine-grained impact analysis resembles the dynamic taint analysis technique, which is proposed to solve and analyze many other security related problems. Many systems [6, 7, 11, 12, 16] detect exploits by tracking the data from untrusted sources such as the network being misused to alter the control flow. Other systems [5, 8, 20] make use of this technique to analyze how sensitive information is processed by the system. Chow et al. applies dynamic taint analysis to understand the lifetime of sensitive information (such as password) in operating systems and large programs [5]. Egele *et al.* utilize this technique to analyze BHO-based spyware behavior [8]. Yin et al. also make use of dynamic taint analysis to detect and analyze privacy-breaching malware [20]. Moreover, dynamic taint analysis is used for other applications, such as automatically extracting protocol message formats [3], and preventing cross-site scripting attacks [19].

5.7 Summary

In this chapter, we presented a novel dynamic analysis approach, *fine-grained impact analysis*, to identify malware hooking behaviors. This approach characterizes malware's impacts on its system environment, and observes if one of the impacts is used to redirect the system execution into the malicious code. Since it captures the intrinsic characteristics of hooking behavior, this technique is able to identify novel hooks. Moreover, we devised a *semantics-aware impact dependency analysis* method to extract the essential information about the hooking mechanisms, which is represented as hook graphs. We developed a prototype, HookFinder, and conducted extensive experiments using representative malware samples from various categories. The experimental results demonstrated that HookFinder can correctly identify the hooking behaviors for all the samples, and the generated hook graphs provide accurate insights about their hooking mechanisms.

References

1. Afxrootkit. http://www.rootkit.com/project.php?id=23
2. Butler, J., Hoglund, G.: VICE–catch the hookers! In: Black Hat USA (2004). http://www. blackhat.com/presentations/bh-usa-04/bh-us-04-butler/bh-us-04-butler.pdf
3. Caballero, J., Yin, H., Liang, Z., Song, D.: Polyglot: Automatic extraction of protocol message format using dynamic binary analysis. In: Proceedings of ACM Conference on Computer and Communication Security (2007)
4. Clandestine file system driver. http://www.rootkit.com/vault/merlvingian/cfsd.zip
5. Chow, J., Pfaff, B., Garfinkel, T., Christopher, K., Rosenblum, M.: Understanding data lifetime via whole system simulation. In: Proceedings of the 13th USENIX Security Symposium (Security'03) (2004)
6. Cost, M., Crowcroft, J., Castro, M., Rowstron, A., Zhou, L., Zhang, L., Barham, P.: Vigilante: End-to-end containment of internet worms. In: 20th ACM Symposium on Operating System Principles (SOSP 2005) (2005)
7. Crandall, J.R., Chong, F.T.: Minos: Control data attack prevention orthogonal to memory model. In: Proceedings of the 37th International Symposium on Microarchitecture (MICRO'04) (2004)
8. Egele, M., Kruegel, C., Kirda, E., Yin, H., Song, D.: Dynamic Spyware Analysis. In: Proceedings of the 2007 Usenix Annual Conference (Usenix'07) (2007)
9. Hacker defender. http://www.rootkit.com/project.php?id=5
10. IceSword. http://www.antirootkit.com/software/IceSword.htm
11. Newsome, J., Song, D.: Dynamic taint analysis for automatic detection, analysis, and signature generation of exploits on commodity software. In: Proceedings of the 12th Annual Network and Distributed System Security Symposium (NDSS) (2005)
12. Portokalidis, G., Slowinska, A., Bos, H.: Argos: an emulator for fingerprinting zero-day attacks. In: EuroSys 2006 (2006)
13. Rutkowska, J.: System virginity verifier: Defining the roadmap for malware detection on windows systems. In: Hack In The Box Security Conference (2005). http://www.invisiblethings. org/papers/hitb05_virginity_verifier.ppt
14. Rutkowska, J.: Rootkit hunting vs. compromise detection. In: Black Hat Federal (2006). http:// www.invisiblethings.org/papers/rutkowska_bhfederal2006.ppt
15. Sony's DRM Rootkit: The Real Story. http://www.schneier.com/blog/archives/2005/11/sonys_drm_rootk.html
16. Suh, G.E., Lee, J.W., Zhang, D., Devadas, S.: Secure program execution via dynamic information flow tracking. In: Proceedings of the 11th International Conference on Architectural Support for Programming Languages and Operating Systems (ASPLOS'04) (2004)
17. UAY kernel-mode backdoor. http://uty.512j.com/uay.rar
18. Vanquish. https://www.rootkit.com/vault/xshadow/vanquish-0.2.1.zip
19. Vogt, P., Nentwich, F., Jovanovic, N., Kirda, E., Kruegel, C., Vigna, G.: Cross-Site Scripting Prevention with Dynamic Data Tainting and Static Analysis. In: Proceeding of the Network and Distributed System Security Symposium (NDSS'07) (2007)
20. Yin, H., Song, D., Egele, M., Kruegel, C., Kirda, E.: Panorama: Capturing system-wide information flow for malware detection and analysis. In: Proceedings of ACM Conference on Computer and Communication Security (2007)

Chapter 6
Analysis of Trigger Conditions and Hidden Behaviors

6.1 Background, Problem Scope and Approach Overview

In many malware programs, certain code paths implementing malicious behaviors will only be executed when certain *trigger conditions* are met [9, 12, 17, 18]. We call such behavior *trigger-based behavior*. Trigger-based behavior may be set off by many different *trigger types*, such as time, system events, and network inputs. For example, many viruses attack their host systems on specific dates, such as Friday the 13th or April Fool's Day [12, 18]; worms may launch attacks at specific times [7], some keyloggers only record keystrokes to files when the application window name contains certain keywords [9]; some browser-helper-object-based spyware only logs information if the URL contains a certain keyword [17]; some distributed denial-of-service tools only start launching attacks when receiving certain network commands [5]. Thus, trigger-based behavior is a real problem, causing millions of dollars of damage [9, 12, 17–21], and detecting trigger-based behavior is important for understanding the malware's malicious behavior and for effective malware defense.

Currently, trigger-based behavior is often analyzed in a tedious, manual process. In this work, we aim to design an approach for automatic trigger-based behavior analysis. We first observe that at a high level, triggers in a program are implemented as conditional jumps depending on inputs from the trigger types of interest such as time, keyboard, or network inputs. The malicious code is triggered when the conditional jumps evaluate to the desired directions, e.g., the current time is equal to the trigger time. Therefore, given trigger types of interest, one key to uncovering trigger-based behavior is to construct values for symbolic inputs (i.e., inputs from trigger types of interest) that makes the conditional jumps evaluate in the desired direction, activating the trigger-dependent code. We call the condition that the symbolic inputs need to satisfy in order for the code execution to go down a path uncovering the trigger-based behavior the *trigger condition*, and the values of the symbolic inputs satisfying the trigger condition the *trigger values*. Second, we observe that trigger-based behavior could be embedded at any point in the program.

H. Yin and D. Song, *Automatic Malware Analysis: An Emulator Based Approach*,
SpringerBriefs in Computer Science, DOI 10.1007/978-1-4614-5523-3_6,
© The Author(s) 2013

Thus, we need to be able to explore many different program paths which could depend on symbolic inputs.

From these observations, we design an approach as a first step towards automatic trigger-based behavior analysis in malware. Our approach takes as inputs the binary program of the malware to be analyzed and a set of trigger types. In order to automatically explore trigger-based behavior in the program based on the given trigger types, we employ *symbolic execution* to automatically and iteratively explore different code paths which could depend on symbolic inputs. In particular, symbolic inputs are represented symbolically, and instructions that depend upon the symbolic inputs operate on symbolic values, and are executed symbolically. Conversely, instructions that do not depend on symbolic inputs operate on concrete values, and are concretely (natively) evaluated (for efficiency). Thus, symbolic execution builds up symbolic formulas over the symbolic inputs (which are in turn based on the trigger types).

6.2 System Design and Implementation

We design and implement a prototype, called *MineSweeper*, to analyze hidden behavior and trigger conditions. We make symbolic execution functionality in TEMU as an important building block.

Trigger Type Specification The user begins analysis by specifying one or more trigger types of interest. Allowing multiple trigger types is necessary because trigger-based behavior may depend on multiple trigger types. For instance, malware may be triggered by a combination of the system time and a keyword in keyboard inputs. By default, MineSweeper provides a list of typical trigger types commonly used in malware, including keyboard inputs, network inputs, the system clock, and other library and system calls used commonly in malware as triggers. In addition, MineSweeper is designed to be easily extensible and allows the user to add additional trigger types. For example, the user can specify any function call or system call as a trigger type.

For each trigger type that the user defines, he needs to specify where in memory the trigger inputs will be stored so that the Mixed Execution Engine can properly assign symbolic variables during mixed execution. For example, if the user specifies the return values of a new function call as a trigger type, he needs to specify where the return values are stored, e.g., in which registers, or the return memory structure of the call or call-by-reference pointers. In our running example, the specification would include that GetLocalTime is a trigger type. The specification would also include that GetLocalTime stores its results in a 16-byte structure pointed to by a stack value when GetLocalTime is called. During mixed execution, this information is used so that a call to GetLocalTime will result in a fresh symbolic variable for each byte returned. Such information is usually readily available in API documentation.

If the user does not know what trigger type the malware may use, they can configure MineSweeper to offer additional assistance. In this case, MineSweeper will monitor the program execution for possible inputs to the program, e.g., system calls and library calls. When a new input source is detected, MineSweeper prompts the user whether the input source should be considered a trigger type of interest.

Symbolic Execution. After trigger types are specified, any inputs of these types will be marked as symbolic. Then we rely on TEMU to perform symbolic execution. That is, TEMU will explore all feasible paths that depend upon these trigger inputs, and solve the path predicate for each of these paths.

6.3 Evaluation

In order to test the effectiveness of our method, we have evaluated Mixed Execution Engine on real malware. Our real world examples include widely spread email worms (NetSky [10] and MyDoom [7]), DDoS tools (TFN [5]), and a keylogger (Perfect Keylogger [15]). All of our experiments were performed on a 2.8Ghz Pentium dual-core processor with 4GB of RAM. Our experiments demonstrate that our techniques are capable of automatically analyzing current real world malware examples. Our experiments also indicate that the total analysis time is quite small compared to an otherwise manual approach.

Results Summary. Table 6.1 shows the results of our experiments. In this table, the "Total Time" column is the total end-to-end experiment time for MineSweeper to analyze each malware, i.e., the time to explore all conditional branches which depend on the trigger inputs. Note that MineSweeper is an unoptimized prototype, and that subsequent optimizations will likely bring the total time down. We break out the total time spent in STP. In our experiments, we spent about 13% time on average solving the path predicates.

The "# Trigger Jumps" column counts how many conditional jumps were based on symbolic inputs. This number is important because it demonstrates that a relatively small number of branches need to be explored in order to uncover the trigger-based behavior in these experiments.

We also show the percent of symbolic vs. number of concrete (x86) instructions executed. These numbers indicate that mixed execution reduces the formula a significant amount. This demonstrates that mixed execution is a promising approach.

Table 6.1 Analysis Results on Real-world Malware Samples using MineSweeper

Program	Total Time	STP Time	Nodes	# Trigger Jumps	Percent Sym. Insn.
MyDoom	28 min	2.2 min	802042	11	0.00136%
NetSky	9 min	0.3 min	119097	6	0.00040%
Perfect Keylogger	2 min	<0.1min	4592	2	0.00508%
TFN	21 min	6.5 min	859759	14	0.00052%

Below we discuss each experiment in more detail.

NetSky. Win32.NetSky is a Win32 worm that spreads via email. The NetSky worm was one of the most widely spread worms of 2004. NetSky is known to have time triggered functionality, however different variants trigger at different times. For example, the C variant is triggered on February 26, 2004 between 6am and 9am [6]. The D variant is triggered on March 2, 2004, when the hour is between 6am and 8am [10]. The NetSky binary we analyzed was packed to prevent static analysis.

In our analysis, MineSweeper output that the library call `GetLocalTime` is a potential trigger type. We specified `GetLocalTime` as the trigger type, which returns a data structure that contains fields for the current month, day, year, hour, and minute. MineSweeper then automatically explored NetSky and analyzed its trigger-based behavior. Figure 6.1 shows a graph of program paths which depend on the trigger. In this graph, node 1 represents the day comparison, node 2 the month, node 3 the year, and nodes 4 through 6 check the hour. As we can see, in order to generate an attack, the date must be February 26, 2004, between 6-9am. According to the Symantec advisory, this is when NetSky.C attacks [6]. We can also see that when the time doesn't match, Netsky will loop back to the beginning and check again.

Overall, MineSweeper was able to discover and uncover the trigger-based behavior in about 9 minutes. We verified that all known trigger-based behavior was discovered.

MyDoom. Win32.MyDoom [7] is another mass-mailing email worm with a built-in denial-of-service time-bomb. Different variants have different trigger dates. All variants launch DDoS attacks, most commonly against www.microsoft.com and www.sco.com. Additionally, most variants contain a termination date which causes them to stop propagating. The MyDoom binary we analyzed was packed. Overall, MineSweeper was able to discover and uncover the trigger-based behavior in MyDoom in about 28 minutes. We verified that all know trigger-based behavior was discovered.

During the initial run, MineSweeper observed that `GetSystemTimeAs Filetime` was a potential trigger type. This library call returns a structure which contains two 32 bit integers representing the current date and time. After adding this specification, MineSweeper discovered MyDoom's behavior depends upon 11 different comparisons with the current date. MineSweeper automatically generated the path predicates, which STP solved. After solving these values, we were able to discover the termination date (Feb 12, 2004) as well as two DDoS dates (Feb 1 and 3, 2004). Feeding these values into the MineSweeper confirmed the DDoS. In addition, these values are confirmed by Symantec as the DDoS dates for MyDoom [7].

Perfect Keylogger. Perfect Keylogger [15] is commercial software that has the ability to trigger itself based on window title (i.e. logging is activated and deactivated by the title of the window that is the target of the keystrokes).

MineSweeper identified `GetWindowTitle` as a possible trigger type. Once we added the trigger type specification, MineSweeper discovered that Perfect Keylogger checks if the current window name contains a pre-configured key string

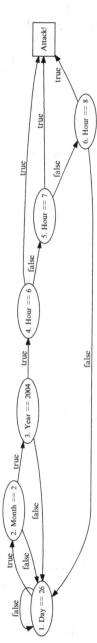

Fig. 6.1 NetSky's Trigger-based Behavior Extracted by MineSweeper

via the strstr library call. In our experiment, we found that MineSweeper branched heavily in the strstr call, e.g., checking if the first byte of the current window name was the same as the key's first byte, then checking if the second byte of the current window name was the same as the key's second byte, etc. In this scenario, MineSweeper continued to make progress, albeit very slowly.

However, since strstr is a standard library function, we can be more efficient by replacing strstr calls with calls to a *summary function*. The summary function concisely summarizes the effects of strstr. Note that summary functions need only be defined once, and can be reused when analyzing other examples, and that they are a widely adopted technique in programming language research [3,22]. Once we added this summary function, MineSweeper was able to quickly discover the trigger value in about 2 minutes. We verified that all know trigger-based behavior was discovered.

TFN: Tribe Flood Network. TFN [5] is a distributed denial-of-service attack zombie. Zombies are often found in the wild where the inner workings are unknown, e.g., the zombie may respond only to unusual messages. In the case of TFN, communication is carried out over ICMP. Different versions of TFN use different maps from command values to actions. Our goal in this experiment is to determine network inputs that would cause TFN to exhibit these different actions.

The original version of TFN that we located was Linux software. For our analysis, we have ported it to Windows since our current implementation is for Windows. Therefore, our version is not vanilla TFN, but it will still allow us to do the relevant analysis.

MineSweeper initially output that a raw ICMP network socket was the trigger type. After adding the appropriate specification, MineSweeper was able to identify and expand 14 conditional jumps that depend on network data. Using the solved formulas that we created, we were able to determine the various command values that this version of TFN would respond to. This complex data was easily generated in only 21 minutes using the MineSweeper system.

6.4 Related Work

Time-bomb analysis. Crandall et al. [4] proposed a virtual-machine-based analysis technique to analyze the timetable of malware. Their technique uses time pertur-bation to identify system timers in Windows. Their technique also uses limited symbolic execution and weakest precondition calculation to identify some time related predicates. This is a good first step towards automatic analysis of time-bombs, however, compared to our holistic approach, their technique does not follow control flow, and can only perform limited symbolic execution, not a full system mixed concrete and symbolic execution. As a result, much of their analysis done in the chapter is manual, and their techniques miss several important time-related predicates. Additionally, while their technique is specialized for time-bombs, ours is designed to support more general trigger types.

Symbolic execution. Symbolic execution was first proposed by King [11]. Recently, symbolic execution has been used for automatic test case generation [8, 16, 23], sound replay of application dialog [14], vulnerability-based signature generation [1].

Mixed execution. DART and EXE have proposed mixed execution for finding bugs in software and have demonstrated that this approach is effective in increasing coverage for automatic testing [2, 8]. Their work is with source code, while ours is with binaries. At a high level, the approaches for mixed execution on source code and binaries are similar in spirit. However, the techniques and engineering of a solution is considerably different. For example, as mentioned one big issue is to deal with the x86 instruction set. Though this may seem like a small side issue, in reality the engineering issues are quite immense. Another difference is source code mixed execution is usually performed by rewriting the source code so that appropriate constraints are generated as it executes. For us, we must perform the instrumentation on the fly.

Moser et al. [13] have independently and concurrently proposed a similar method of exploring multiple paths in a binary using symbolic execution. They have also demonstrated positive results using this approach. While our approach is similar, our system is capable of handling bit-level operations and more complicated, nonlinear formulas for symbolic variables within the system.

6.5 Summary

We have proposed that automatically analyzing trigger-based behavior in malware is possible, and designed and implemented a system using mixed execution as a first step towards this goal. Since often trigger-based analysis of malware is manual, any help provided by MineSweeper is of great use. In our experiments with real-world malware, we demonstrate MineSweeper is capable of:

- Detecting the existence of trigger-based behavior for specified trigger types;
- Finding the trigger condition;
- Find input values that satisfy the trigger condition, when the trigger condition can be solved;
- Feeding the trigger values to the program, causing it to exhibit the trigger-based behavior, so that it may be analyzed in a controlled environment.

Even when automatic analysis fails, MineSweeper can provide an analyst with valuable information about potential trigger-based behavior: information which previously would have to be manually obtained. Automatic trigger-based behavior detection is a challenging task, and we hope our work sheds new light and encourages further work in this area.

References

1. Brumley, D., Newsome, J., Song, D., Wang, H., Jha, S.: Towards automatic generation of vulnerability-based signatures. In: Proceedings of the 2006 IEEE Symposium on Security and Privacy, pp. 2–16 (2006)
2. Cadar, C., Ganesh, V., Pawlowski, P., Dill, D., Engler, D.: EXE: A system for automatically generating inputs of death using symbolic execution. In: Proceedings of the 13th ACM Conference on Computer and Communications Security (CCS) (2006)
3. Clarke, E., Kroening, D., Lerda, F.: A tool for checking ANSI-C programs. In: K. Jensen, A. Podelski (eds.) Tools and Algorithms for the Construction and Analysis of Systems (TACAS 2004), *Lecture Notes in Computer Science*, vol. 2988, pp. 168–176. Springer (2004)
4. Crandall, J.R., Wassermann, G., de Oliveira, D.A.S., Su, Z., Wu, S.F., Chong, F.T.: Temporal search: Detecting hidden malware timebombs with virtual machines. In: Proceedings of the 12th International Conference on Architectural Support for Programming Languages and Operating Systems, ASPLOS-XII, pp. 25–36 (2006)
5. Dittrich, D.: The "tribe flood network" distributed denial of service attack tool. http://staff.washington.edu/dittrich/misc/tfn.analysis.txt (1999)
6. Ferrie, T.L.: Win32.Netsky.C. http://www.symantec.com/security_response/writeup.jsp?docid=2004-022417-4628-99
7. Gettis, S.: W32.Mydoom.B@mm. http://www.symantec.com/security_response/writeup.jsp?docid=2004-022011-2447-99
8. Godefroid, P., Klarlund, N., Sen, K.: DART: Directed automated random testing. In: Proc. of the 2005 Programming Language Design and Implementation Conference (PLDI) (2005)
9. Ha, K.: Keylogger.Stawin. http://www.symantec.com/security_response/writeup.jsp?docid=2004-012915-2315-99
10. Hindocha, N.: Win32.Netsky.D. http://www.symantec.com/security_response/writeup.jsp?docid=2004-030110-0232-99
11. King, J.: Symbolic execution and program testing. Communications of the ACM **19**, 386–394 (1976)
12. McAfee: W97M/Opey.C. ttp://vil.nai.com/vil/content/v_10290.htm
13. Moser, A., Kruegel, C., Kirda, E.: Exploring multiple execution paths for malware analysis. In: Proceedings of the 2007 IEEE Symposium on Security and Privacy(Oakland'07) (2007)
14. Newsome, J., Brumley, D., Franklin, J., Song, D.: Replayer: Automatic protocol replay by binary analysis. In: R. Write, S.D.C. di Vimercati, V. Shmatikov (eds.) In the Proceedings of the 13th ACM Conference on Computer and and Communications Security (CCS), pp. 311–321 (2006)
15. Blazingtools perfect keylogger. http://www.blazingtools.com/bpk.html
16. Sen, K., Marinov, D., Agha, G.: CUTE: A concolic unit testing engine for c. In: ACM SIGSOFT Sympsoium on the Foundations of Software Engineering (2005)
17. Symantec: Spyware.e2give. http://www.symantec.com/security_response/writeup.jsp?docid=2004-102614-1006-99
18. Symantec: Xeram.1664. http://www.symantec.com/security_response/writeup.jsp?docid=2000-121913-2839-99
19. United States Department of Justice Press Release: Former computer network administrator at new jersey high-tech firm sentenced to 41 months for unleashing $10 million computer "time bomb". http://www.usdoj.gov/criminal/cybercrime/lloydSent.htm
20. United States Department of Justice Press Release: Former lance, inc. employee sentenced to 24 months and ordered to pay $194,609 restitution in computer fraud case. http://www.usdoj.gov/criminal/cybercrime/SullivanSent.htm

21. United States Department of Justice Press Release: Former technology manager sentenced to a year in prison for computer hacking offense. http://www.usdoj.gov/criminal/cybercrime/sheaSent.htm
22. Xie, Y., Aiken, A.: Context- and path-sensitive memory leak detection. ACM SIGSOFT Software Engineering Notes **30** (2005)
23. Yang, J., Sar, C., Twohey, P., Cadar, C., Engler, D.: Automatically generating malicious disks using symbolic execution. In: IEEE Symposium on Security and Privacy (2006)

Chapter 7
Concluding Remarks

7.1 Discussion and Future Work

Everything has limitations. So is the techniques described in this book. Here, we systematically discuss several limitations. Furthermore, we discuss some counter-measures and pointers to future research.

7.1.1 Detecting, Evading and Subverting the Analysis Platform

Malware can detect the discrepancies between the emulated environment and real execution platform. After detecting the presence of our analysis platform, malware may choose to evade or subvert it. Some study shows the possibility of subverting the entire emulated environment by exploiting buffer overflows and integer bugs [9]. Therefore, we need to fix these bugs to prevent the subversion attacks.

Malware can detect the presence of QEMU/TEMU in a variety of ways [5, 10]. First, malware can check the hardware characteristics. QEMU emulates a set of hardware devices, some of which are unique. However, this detection vector will also catch virtual machines that use the same set of hardware devices (such as Xen [12] and KVM [6]). Given that virtual machines are gaining more and more popularity on personal computers and production systems, this detection vector will not work effectively in practice. Second, malware can check the timing differences. This detection vector exploits the fact that an operation will take a different amount of time (most likely longer time) under emulation than on real hardware. Third, malware may target CPU instructions whose behaviors in an emulated system differ from their behaviors in real hardware. Martignoni et al. conducted automatic fuzzing test on numeric system emulators and showed that QEMU performs differently than real CPU on hundreds of unique test cases [7]. Each of them could be used to detect the presence of QEMU.

H. Yin and D. Song, *Automatic Malware Analysis: An Emulator Based Approach*,
SpringerBriefs in Computer Science, DOI 10.1007/978-1-4614-5523-3_7,
© The Author(s) 2013

To address the transparency issue, Dinaburg et al. proposed a malware analysis framework, called Ether, which leverages hardware virtualization extension (e.g., Intel-VT and AMD-V) [2]. Ether effectively hides timing differences by factoring out extra time for analysis operations, and gets ride of CPU semantics differences by executing directly on native CPU. Therefore, Ether provides excellent transparency. However, hardware virtualization does not offer a good foundation for fine-grained binary analysis. Although the single-step mode in CPU enables instruction-level instrumentation, its performance overhead is significantly higher than that of a system emulator (at least 5 times in our experiment). This is because in single-step mode, each instruction triggers a hardware interrupt. Moreover, emulators like QEMU break down each complex instruction into intermediate operations. Reasoning on these intermediate operations is substantially easier than directly on instructions. Unfortunately, Ether does not have this support.

A promising approach to a transparent fine-grained extensible malware analysis platform would be combining emulator technique with hardware virtualization technique, for example by record and replay. That is, we can first run malware in a hardware-assisted virtual machine and record hardware inputs and other critical events. Then we replay these hardware inputs and events in a whole-system emulator to perform fine-grained malware analysis. Chow et al. have demonstrated the feasibility of recording hardware inputs in VMWare and replaying these inputs in QEMU [1]. By literally replaying CPU tick counts, detecting timing differences are effectively eliminated. Detecting CPU semantics differences can also be addressed by efficiently locating divergence points during replay. Indeed, such a system was recently proposed to build an extensible and transparent malware analysis platform by combining hardware virtualization and software emulation [13].

7.1.2 Limitations of Dynamic Analysis

An open problem for dynamic analysis lies in its limited test coverage. Malware may evade detection and analysis by simply not performing malicious behavior during the dynamic analysis. It may stay inactive until certain conditions are satisfied. For example, time bombs activate themselves only on specific dates, and some keyloggers only record keystrokes for certain applications or windows. In Chapter 6, we address this problem by specifying certain inputs as symbolic, and automatically exploring multiple execution paths. Moser et al. also implemented a similar idea [8]. However, there are several limitations with this technique. First, we cannot predict all trigger conditions and mark them as symbolic. In practice, we only treat some common inputs as symbolic, such as system time, the availability of internet connection, the existence of certain registry keys, and filesystem and network inputs. If some malicious behaviors depend on certain trigger conditions that are not monitored, it is unlikely to disclose and analyze these malicious behaviors. Second, this technique does not scale. The number of execution paths to be explored increases exponentially with the increase of symbolic inputs.

Malware writer can exploit this limitation by making the control flow graph arbitrarily large and complex. In consequence, our analysis would run out of resources before reaching the actual malicious behaviors.

Another problem is denial-of-service attacks to dynamic analysis, especially to fine-grained dynamic analysis techniques discussed in this book. Fine-grained dynamic analysis requires substantially more CPU and storage resources than native execution. Malware writers can exploit this fact to launch a denial-of-service attack. Embedded with expensive operations (such as time lock puzzles [3]), the malicious code can effectively render malware analysis systems to run out of resources and time.

Solutions to these two problems will be interesting research topics. For example, we could significantly improve the performance of fine-grained analysis techniques by having better hardware support or better software optimization.

7.1.3 Limitations of Taint Analysis

In this book, we take advantage of taint analysis technique to keep track of information flow in a fine-grained manner. However, taint analysis is not a panacea. Conservative taint analysis may lead to taint explosion, and attackers may evade taint analysis though implicit flows. How to address these two limitations will be important future work.

Taint Explosion. Taint analysis is conservative in tracking data flow. In an arithmetic operation, if any byte of inputs is tainted, we mark all bytes of the output to be tainted. In order to keep track of taint through conversion table lookups, we also extend taint analysis policy to propagate taint if the index for a memory read becomes tainted. As shown in Slowinska et al.'s study [11], this naive approach will leave to taint explosion very soon. In Panorama, we mitigate this taint explosion problem by using a heuristic policy: tainting through table lookups is only allowed up to a configurable number of times, starting from its taint source. The rationale behind this is that there are only a small number of table lookups (e.g., less than 3) for legitimate purposes. A tainted value derived through a large number of table lookups is unlikely to be strongly related to the taint source. In practice, we found this heuristic policy effectively mitigate taint explosion. However, it may introduce false negatives. Moreover, malicious code may exploit this policy to break taint analysis by introducing a large number of table lookups.

Implicit Information Flow. Taint analysis keeps track of information propagating through direct data dependency. It is worth noting that information may also propagate through other channels, such as control flow dependency. This situation does not happen very often in benign program, but a malicious program could exploit implicit information flow to conceal the fact that sensitive information is leaked. Researchers have proposed to extend taint analysis to track control flow dependency by computing control flow graph and tainting outputs between the predominator and the post-dominator [4]. This scheme does not solve this problem successfully for two reasons. First, it does not track the outputs generated in unvisited paths between the predominator and the post dominator. The attackers can construct some code snippet to propagate information through these unvisited paths. Thus, this scheme is incomplete. Second, this extension can become another major factor for taint explosion.

7.2 Conclusion

In this book, we sought to capture the intrinsic natures in malicious behaviors, in order to build more effective automatic malware analysis systems. Malware analysis is likely the most challenging problem in binary code analysis. To address the common challenges, we proposed a new architecture for binary analysis, and implemented a unified and extensible analysis platform, called TEMU. We proposed a core technique, namely layered annotative execution, as a Swiss army knife for fine-grained dynamic binary analysis, and implemented this technique in TEMU. Then on the basis of TEMU, we proposed and built a series of novel techniques for automatic malware analysis. More concretely, we have developed *Renovo*, *Panorama*, *HookFinder*, and *MineSweeper*, for detecting and analyzing various aspects of malware. we believe that our techniques are effective and practical. Moreover, since these techniques capture intrinsic characteristics of malware, they are well suited for dealing with new malware samples and attack mechanisms.

We also systematically discussed several fundamental limitations in our proposed techniques. More concretely, we pointed out that although our analysis platform is better suited for analyzing malicious code than the other conventional ones (e.g., debugger and disassembler), malware authors may still find ways to detect and evade it. Moreover, an open problem for dynamic analysis lies in its limited test coverage. Finally, as a core analysis technique, dynamic taint analysis has several limitations, including taint explosion and implicit information flow. Such discussions shed light on future directions for automatic malware analysis.

References

1. Chow, J., Garfinkel, T., Chen, P.M.: Decoupling dynamic program analysis from execution in virtual environments. In: USENIX 2008 Annual Technical Conference, pp. 1–14 (2008)
2. Dinaburg, A., Royal, P., Sharif, M., Lee, W.: Ether: malware analysis via hardware virtualization extensions. In: Proceedings of the 15th ACM Conference on Computer and Communications Security, pp. 51–62 (2008)
3. Ebringer, T.: Anti-emulation through time-lock puzzles. http://www.datasecurity-event.com/uploads/timelock.pdf
4. Egele, M., Kruegel, C., Kirda, E., Yin, H., Song, D.: Dynamic Spyware Analysis. In: Proceedings of the 2007 Usenix Annual Conference (Usenix'07) (2007)

5. Ferrie, P.: Attacks on virtual machine emulators. Symantec Security Response (2006)
6. Kernel-based virtual machine. http://www.linux-kvm.org/
7. Martignoni, L., Paleari, R., Roglia, G.F., Bruschi, D.: Testing CPU emulators. In: Proceedings of the 2009 International Conference on Software Testing and Analysis (ISSTA), Chicago, Illinois, U.S.A. ACM (2009)
8. Moser, A., Kruegel, C., Kirda, E.: Exploring multiple execution paths for malware analysis. In: Proceedings of the 2007 IEEE Symposium on Security and Privacy(Oakland'07) (2007)
9. Ormandy, T.: An Empirical Study into the Security Exposure to Host of Hostile Virtualized Environments. http://taviso.decsystem.org/virtsec.pdf
10. Raffetseder, T., Krügel, C., Kirda, E.: Detecting system emulators. In: Information Security, 10th International Conference, ISC 2007, pp. 1–18 (2007)
11. Slowinska, A., Bos, H.: Pointless tainting? evaluating the practicality of pointer tainting. In: Proceedings of ACM SIGOPS EUROSYS. Nuremberg, Germany (2009)
12. Xen. http://www.xen.org/
13. Yan, L.K., Jayachandra, M., Zhang, M., Yin, H.: V2E: Combining hardware virtualization and software emulation for transparent and extensible malware analysis. In: Proceedings of the Eighth Annual International Conference on Virtual Execution Environments (VEE'12) (2012)